# THE GOLFING BODYMIND

# THE GOLFING BODYMIND

Sandy Dunlop

WILDWOOD HOUSE LONDON

*To Shivas Irons*

First published in Great Britain 1980

Wildwood House Limited
1 Prince of Wales Passage
117 Hampstead Road
London NW1 3EE

In Australia by Bookwise Australia Pty Ltd,
104 Sussex Street, Sydney, 2000.



ISBN 0 7045 3029 5

The photographs in the illustrated section
are provided by kind permission of
The Keystone Press Agency Ltd. The
close-up of Tony Jacklin is copyright
© John Leatherbarrow, Farington.

Typeset by Saildean Ltd, Surrey
Printed and bound in Great Britain by
Biddles Ltd, Guildford

# CONTENTS

PART THREE SOME IMPLICATIONS



## ACKNOWLEDGEMENTS

This book owes much to three great 'systems' thinkers. The first was a man who could neither read nor write and yet who was able to communicate all the ideas in this book in a language that all could understand and with great humour. That man was Andra Kirkaldy, the great St. Andrews golf professional, who learnt all he needed to know about people and about life from his profession. Each chapter of this book begins with a quote from Andra's book (dictated to a friend) *My Fifty Years of Golf: Memoirs.*

The second systems thinker was a controversial, self-taught Australian who developed a method of mind-body re-education known as the Alexander technique. This was F. M. Alexander, who was writing, like Kirkaldy, fifty years ago and stressing the importance of mind and body in the golf game and how we placed too much emphasis on the techniques of the game.

The third character is Michael Murphy, the author of my golfing bible *Golf in the Kingdom*, and one who was a product of the best of Western education, Stanford University. It seems the ability to look at the 'whole' rather than merely the parts is not exclusive to a particular background.

I must also thank my mother and sister for their tremendous support during a lonely year in my room in Bristol. Janet, Becca and Heather did an excellent job typing the manuscript. I would particularly like to thank Maureen Lockhart for her advice on the Yoga Breathing Exercises, Appendix II . Finally, I'd like to thank the two editors, Kim and Oliver. I'd especially like to thank them both for their patience and Oliver for his funny letters.

# *Chapter One*

## INTRODUCTION TO THE SYSTEMS APPROACH

*'Every golfer knows that the reading of books telling him how to play very often puts him off his game, and very seldom does him much good.'*

There are innumerable books which advise golfers how to improve their game by modifying or changing this or that aspect of their technique. This is not another such book. On the contrary, it is intended to show how, by adopting a new attitude and developing a new understanding of the relationship between mind and body, and of the mental and emotional aspects of the game, golfers may improve their play and derive greater enjoyment from it. This is the result of the application of Systems Theory and other related 'holistic' approaches. Although these philosophies may seem somewhat remote from the golf course, I hope to show that they are, in fact, very relevant to the game.

Golf, as most top players admit, is a 'mental' game, yet this aspect of the game is rarely given serious attention by authors or teaching professionals and seldom considered in any depth by the golfer himself. This book is intended not merely to redress this neglect of the mental side of the game, but to propose a 'synthesis' which includes its physical, mental and emotional dimensions.

And included in this synthesis is the conventional approach to golf improvement which aims at technical perfection. Technique is, of course, a basic requirement and particularly in the early stages. However, once this is adequate the golfer should begin to consider what I propose to call 'the golfing bodymind'. It is in this area that Systems Theory, the Alexander Principle, yoga, zen and other related methods can help. All of these methods are 'holistic' approaches to the bodymind, with the exception of Systems Theory which is the science of holistic organization. However, I propose to show that it, too, can be adapted to the human system.

These methods can help because they provide some excellent clues to how the golfer can develop the abilities to handle the pressures that face us all on the course. They can also help in that they are techniques which are designed to move us towards our true potential or fulfilment. Handling golfing crises and reaching our potential are obviously closely related and are matters which make it clear that the Systems approach to the golfing bodymind is very concerned with our peak golfing moments.

One of the effects of developing a greater understanding of the golfing bodymind is an increase in the enjoyment derived from the game. In the competitive golfing world people think far more in terms of winning and results; it is perhaps an anathema to mention enjoyment which is rarely given the consideration it merits. This is a pity, because for someone who plays the game competitively, enjoyment is very closely related to fulfilling their potential at the game. Enjoyment goes hand in hand with the knowledge that you are doing your best and for this reason it is an important dimension of the argument presented here.

The other central theme of this book is that as golfers we should develop the ability to handle those crises that crop up for us all, no matter at what level we play. The touring professional is obviously faced with intense pressure as a tournament draws to a close, but this pressure is little different from that faced by the club player, who often has considerably less golfing skill with which to handle it. Crises of a slightly different kind also occur during stroke play rounds: say when you have dropped two shots and are faced with a tricky five foot putt. To hole the putt would mean getting back in the game. You are also well aware that such a make or break point has been reached and furthermore that certain golfers always come up with what is needed whereas others almost always fail.

My argument is that whether you are one of those who succeeds or fails in situations like these is not merely a matter of luck or fate. It is no accident that Gary Player can fight back from seven down to beat Tony Lema in the Piccadilly. It is no accident that he wins the 1978 U.S. Masters after being seven shots back going in to the final round and then does it again in two successive tournaments. You can develop the ability to handle crises. What really matters in a crisis on the course is what is going on in your golfing body and golfing mind. This 'crunch situation' is not asking for the details of your grip or stance; it is asking about your inner resources, because it is these and only these that will give you the strength to pull through. The golfing crisis is a very lonely experience. This book is concerned with what it takes to handle this experience.

*The Systems Approach*

This emphasis on the peak or crisis moment on the golf course is very much the result of the starting point taken by Systems Theory. Whereas the conventional approach to golfing problems would begin by asking, somewhat negatively, about the golfer's technical errors and then attempt to look for solutions, the Systems approach asks about qualities which enable the golfer to survive and adapt in his characteristic environment – in this case the world of the top class professional golfer. And it is necessary to ask which of these qualities are exhibited by those who do survive in this highly competitive world. What do the top golfers themselves isolate as being the basis of their success under pressure?

The one quality that the professional would isolate above all others is *concentration.* As Tommy Bolt says, 'Once you learn to play championship golf, concentration is seventy-five per cent of how well you do it.'[1] Arnold Palmer was once asked what he thought he did best. His reply was 'concentrate'. For Ben Hogan 'an ability to concentrate for long periods of time while exposed to all sorts of distractions is invaluable in golf'.[2] It is, clearly, a matter of central importance and will, therefore, constitute one of the Systems qualities which all be considered in some depth.

A second quality relates to temperament and 'keeping your head while all around are losing theirs'. What is needed is the ability to remain in the same controlled mood regardless of what is happening to you or to others. Every round ever played has its good and bad moments but the golfer must avoid going up and down with these different circumstances. He must develop the ability to remain in control.

Gary Player makes the point very clearly in his autobiography when he talks of two of the world's outstanding golfers:

> Bobby Locke was a golfer with an amazingly even temperament. He did everything quietly and in slow motion. It didn't make any difference whether he was playing in a tournament, driving a car or changing his shoes in the locker room, Bobby moved slowly, but every motion had a purpose. He just refused to get upset about anything or rush around in a flurry. And I'm convinced that's one reason at least why he was such an outstanding golfer.

and

[1] *Golf Digest* October 1971.
[2] Ibid.

> 'Jack Nicklaus is a marvel when it comes to temperament. In fact I think he has the most even disposition of any human being who's ever played golf. Even when Jack is hitting the ball poorly I've seen him come off the course with a 68. The secret is his ability to always remain calm and on an even keel. By keeping cool he's usually able to convert an almost disastrous or impossible situation into an asset.'[1]

The one word that describes this quality is *equanimity*, a quality which relates principally to the emotional side of the game. It is, however, most closely related to tempo and rhythm with which all golfers are familiar. The importance of the concept was stressed by the note Tom Weiskopf left in Tony Jacklin's locker just before he went out to win the 1969 British Open Championship. It contained one word – 'tempo'. It was a reminder to Jacklin to avoid the tendency to speed up his swing under pressure. However, tempo and rhythm are closely related to the golfer's state of mind. They are merely the physical manifestation of fear and tension. By attacking this mental and emotional side of the problem we are getting to the underlying cause.

A final quality is *awareness*. As a rule golfers tend not to think about this quality. It is, nevertheless, extremely relevant in any attempt to gain control of the golfing mind, body and emotions, a control which must be seen as an essential prerequisite to fulfilling your golfing potential. Timothy Gallwey stresses the physical dimension of awareness very well in the following passage:

> In our culture relatively little importance has been given to body awareness. Yet it is only those athletes who have highly developed kinesthetic sense – muscle sense – who ever achieve high levels of excellence. One simply can't play any sport well lacking the ability to focus carefully on the subtle body sensations which indicate the difference between balance and off-balance, timing and mis-timing, too tight and too loose. Body awareness is directly related to body achievement.[2]

This body awareness is, of course, particularly relevant and is usually called 'feel'. It also becomes progressively more important the closer the golfer gets to the hole. The success of a delicate chip over the bunker to win a match depends far more on feel than technique. The reason the Japanese have a reputation for having superb short games is surely because theirs is a culture which understands the importance of awareness of subtle movements of

[1] Gary Player *Gary Player, World Golfer*, p. 57
[2] T. Gallwey *Inner Tennis*, p. 74

the muscles of the body. Oriental disciplines such as Tai Chi and Aikido stress and teach this awareness.

The mental and emotional dimensions of the concept of awareness also deserve consideration because of their relevance to the understanding and training of the golfing bodymind. For example, training yourself to become aware quickly of the fact that you are not concentrating is a good means of improving concentration. Further, the emotions felt on the golf course can only be controlled and integrated if they are recognized, fully experienced and understood.

We have, then, isolated the three Systems qualities of concentration, equanimity and awareness. They are the qualities that stand out once the technical side of the game has been mastered to a satisfactory degree. They are what really matter when the pressure increases on the course and will consequently occupy a very central place in my argument.

*Internal Solutions*

There is one significant and overriding aspect of this Systems approach to the golfing bodymind which must be understood: the tendency we all have of making excuses for our failings. We blame the weather, the greens, the playing partners, the clubs – in fact, anything and everything.

The Systems approach rejects absolutely this excuse-making: you as a 'golfing system' are *responsible* for your actions regardless of what they are. If you take an 88 you are responsible for it in the same way you are responsible for a 68. The real point is that the external factors are there whether you like it or not. You cannot change them. All you as a golfer can do is to change your reactions to them.

Another aspect of this tendency to look without rather than within, is that we search continuously for external solutions to our golfing problems. This is no doubt due partly to the commercial concerns who like to have us believe that our problems will disappear if we purchase their particular balls, clubs or trousers. We also search endlessly for that miracle gimmick, tip or lesson that can suddenly transform us.

The Systems view is that there are seldom easy solutions to the more important golfing problems and that these are to be found in your golfing body and your golfing mind. It is the recognition of this fact and acceptance of personal responsibility for your golfing acts that is the starting point on the road towards your true golfing potential. The road may well lead to the profound realization that there is something behind Shivas Irons' assertion that 'the basis for a change in the way a person plays the game must be laid in his entire life'.[1]

### *The Structure*

With our three Systems qualities in mind the book will start by examining various traditional approaches to golf. Some of these approaches such as the Alexander Technique, psychosynthesis and zen will not be familiar to most golfers but have, nonetheless, been suggested over the last fifty years by writers on golf who recognized the necessity of considering the golfing mind and body when seeking to understand the problems of the golf course. They looked for underlying causes. The first section will conclude with an attempt to draw these techniques together within the Systems framework which underlies the book.

The second and third sections of the book introduce and develop further the Systems approach. After a brief and non-technical introduction to the new, evolving science of Systems Theory, the three Systems qualities will be considered in greater detail. In the second section several practical methods which can be used to develop these Systems qualities will be considered. The third section of the book will take a practical approach and consider what a Systems future might suggest for the golfer both on and off the course. Different aspects of the game such as the practice session and the golf lesson will be looked at critically and with a view to providing some fresh insights.

[1] M. Murphy *Golf in the Kingdom*, p. 157. Shivas Irons is the wise Scottish golf professional who features in Michael Murphy's book. Shivas was a great 'Systems thinker' and taught his pupils the mysteries of the inner game of golf.

# *Part One*

# TRADITIONAL APPROACHES

# *Chapter Two*

# THE SEARCH FOR PERFECTION

*'It is extremely easy to attach too much importance to what might be called the "fine points" of the game.'*

As already mentioned, this book is not about the physical mechanics of the game. There have apparently been over two thousand books published on that subject[1] and a quick review of golfing periodicals reveals that at least half of their space is devoted to this type of instructional material. It is a search directed towards the perfection of the technical side of the game and is likely to continue.

Nor is this book intended to add anything to the multitude of different theories and methods. What is proposed is to make certain suggestions/criticisms which are an attempt to look at the conventional approach to golf from a Systems perspective. These criticisms will, it is hoped, clarify the relationship between the technical approach that has been adopted to date and the holistic methods that are to be suggested. This relationship should be seen very much as a marriage, a synthesis. The two approaches are complementary. Indeed, reaching your full potential will not be possible if either has been neglected.

*Systems Suggestions*

The one thing that a Systems approach to the technical side of golf stresses is the importance of stepping back and looking at your game as a whole, appreciating that 'the parts' – grip, swing, stance, posture and so on – are not separate and disconnected but different

[1] See David Morley *The Missing Links* – one of the very few books concentrating on the mental aspects of the game.

aspects of a totality which must work as such, smoothly and harmoniously. If they do not 'mesh' together, your game will suffer.

The books and articles sometimes overlook this vital point. Even if you have technical flaws it is quite possible to build in compensations to balance them. Lee Trevino is a good example of a player who has accomplished this. Also, having a clear idea of the swing as a whole is quite likely to make the particular weakness unimportant.

One situation in which it is very important to have a clear idea of the whole is when you are in a really difficult spot in the course. For example, in the tight or sandy lies around the green, when it is too easy to become obsessed and worried about just one aspect of the shot, like the contact the club will make with the ball. The failure to think of where and how the ball will go or of the appropriate swing, usually leads to disastrous results.

A second suggestion implied by the Systems approach is that the golfer should be prepared for these crisis shots on the course. The young Spanish caddies understand this. They spend hours practising chip shots off roads, paths and 'impossible' lies. As a result golfers like Severiano Ballesteros have superb short games. The point is that the margin for error on these 'impossible' shots is minute. They have to be perfect, whereas an easy shot can be effective even if miss-hit. Another effect of this over-training is that when faced with an easy shot in reality it becomes easier. Also pulling off an impossible shot can do wonders for the confidence. There is clearly much wisdom in the training for the crisis shot even if it is rarely needed. One final bit of Systems wisdom relates to the crucial problem of assimilating the vast number of theories and tips available. This plethora of information tends to lead to an obsession with techniques. As F.E. Emery points out: 'Co-ordination and control become ends in themselves. They are not seen in their full perspective as adjusting the system to its environment but as desirable goals.'[1]

So perfecting your golf technique must always be seen as a means towards your golfing goals and not as a goal in itself. Don't become obsessed with theory. A second point is to avoid the tendency to interpret *all* your golfing ailments in technical terms. Some, as will be seen below, have little or nothing to do with technique.

On the technical side of the game the problem is really two-fold. Either the golfer suffers from too much information or from too little. This latter category is not receptive to new ideas or to advice from either friends or professionals. Those in the former category

[1] F. E. Emery *Systems Thinking*, p. 101

listen to all advice, try it all and end up in a complete mess. The top golfer, on the other hand, is always receptive to advice but, more importantly, he can sift the good from the bad and only lets in what is relevant and helpful. He has a vital, but little appreciated, discriminatory skill regarding the technical side of the game.

Self-regulation is no easy thing to acquire. It is the result of experience, practice and intelligent study of your game – which is hard work. This concept of self-regulation must be borne in mind during any work on the technical, mechanical side of golf whether of a practical or theoretical nature. The role of the teacher of technique is thus to make himself redundant.

*Some Systems Criticisms*

Systems Theory provides the basis for some valuable and incisive criticisms of the conventional approach to golf. First the failure to recognize (or the overlooking of) the real causes of many of our golfing problems. Often these lie far deeper than is sometimes realized and nothing is more frustrating than trying to cure a fault with remedies that are themselves faulty – the product of superficial diagnosis. For example, if you slice a ball the real cause may be failure to concentrate because of domestic or business worries, rather than an easily corrected technical error. If the diagnosis is incorrect, the suggested remedy will merely compound the problem or lead to new symptoms of the unresolved underlying malaise.

People with golf problems can be driven slowly to despair and frustration through faulty diagnosis and faulty remedies. Things can become so bad that the unfortunate golfer abandons the game altogether. While this may be the best thing to cure the problem which can now be seen in perspective – holistically – it is a pity to suffer the anguish and despair.

Thus the real cause of your golfing problems, the real obstacles to achieving your full potential as a player, may lie somewhere in your life beyond the golf course, or in your relationship with your body, or in some aspect of your 'inner self'. And no complete diagnosis can be expected to emerge from conventional coaching or from conventional attitudes to the sport.

Systems diagnosis can help the golfer who swings too quickly, knows he does and yet, seemingly, can do nothing about it. What this golfer needs is to take a critical look at the rest of his life. Does he, for instance, rush around like a madman all day? Is he taking out on the golf ball the frustration he feels towards life generally and, in particular, his own life? Does he feel a failure?

For the golfer interested in this approach the following chapters provide some insight into how he might look critically at his game from a wider, overall perspective. And if you, as a golfer, feel that you have never quite become what you can become, you might find in these different techniques and disciplines some possible explanations.

There is one other significant criticism of the conventional approach to golf. It is this: the search for the perfect technique is *bound to fail.* There is a characteristic common to all living systems, that of *equifinality.* This principle states that a system can reach the same final state from differing initial conditions and by a variety of paths. Lee Trevino and Doug Sanders are two players who would agree with this concept.

In golf this principle implies that there is no one perfect way to play but there is a best way for each individual. There is also a best way for you at each stage in your golfing evolution; it is a way that is dynamic – it changes over time.

Admittedly, as a player approaches his peak, the nearer he or she gets to complete control over every aspect of the game, the number of different approaches will be reduced. Also, the greater the skill and control, the fewer the variations in attitude or technique that are possible or permissable. Systems language says that as 'the system' gains greater control in its operations the amount of equifinality may be reduced.[1] These words '*may be* reduced' are very significant. The point being that you, as a golfer, do not have to get closer and closer to some ideal as you approach your true potential. You may even move away from it! There is no such thing as a perfect swing for all golfers, and there never will be – even if another two thousand books are written on the subject. There will, however, always be *a best way for you,* but it is you and only you who must find it.

SUMMARY

This chapter has looked critically at the conventional approach to golf, and attempted to make several positive suggestions and comments from the Systems viewpoint. Both approaches must be seen as complementary. The 'holistic' must be combined with the 'partial' at all stages in the golfer's evolution. Systems qualities such as concentration and equanimity do not suddenly become evident after mastering the mechanics of golf. They must be worked upon. In fact, these qualities are probably more difficult to master than technique and they certainly do not appear after half an hour with a golf professional!

[1] Katz and Kahn in F. E. Emery *Systems Thinking*, p. 100

The Systems message is: you must take steps to acquire all the essential qualities, including both the technical and the Systems qualities. All your efforts will be in vain if you haven't the strength to handle the situation you are striving to overcome, if you are not ready for the crisis when it arrives. There is a world of difference between actually reaching the top of Mount Everest and having to turn back a few hundred feet from the summit. Don't forget it will become harder and harder. The environment asks more and more of the system.

So while neither tells the whole story, the Systems approach argues that it is ultimately the crucial one. The Systems qualities are the most difficult to develop. They come as a result of sustained and determined effort. For this reason they must be developed all through your golfing evolution. In the end, little else will be important!

# *Chapter Three*

# THE PHYSICAL SIDE – SUGGESTED APPROACHES

*'Not by strength but by art.'*

There is a difference of opinion amongst those who speak or write on golf, as to whether physical exercise benefits the serious golfer. While the great Gary Player argues strongly in favour of exercise, and is indeed living proof of its benefits, another lesser-known golfing writer has produced impressive reasons why conventional exercise systems are likely to have an adverse effect. He is F. Matthias Alexander, an Australian actor, who developed a technique which has become known as the 'Alexander Principle'.

### *Against Exercise – the Alexander Principle*

Most golfers will not be familiar with 'the Alexander Principle'. This is a pity, because his work and some subsequent interpretations offer excellent insight into the workings of the golfing bodymind. Alexander gives useful and original explanations of what are probably the two most common golfing problems – 'mind-wandering' and 'head up'. The work is thus clearly so relevant that, since it was first published some fifty years ago, it is somewhat surprising that there has been no widespread application of the Principle amongst the golfing fraternity.

Before discussing some of Alexander's main arguments and considering his criticism of conventional exercise techniques, it is necessary to introduce briefly his interesting theory of evolution.

The basis of Alexander's theory was his vision of all behaviour in terms of an INPUT-THROUGHPUT-OUTPUT (I.T.O.) sequence. The input is the stimulus that our bodymind receives from the environment and the output is the response. The throughput is the conscious control applied prior to any output or response. This approach, incidentally, is identical to a Systems analysis of our problems.

The first stage of evolution Alexander called the *Uncivilized Stage* – when the I.T.O. sequence worked satisfactorily because Man had a bodymind on which he could rely. He had a highly developed state of sensory appreciation and co-ordination comparable to the animals which surrounded him. He could therefore trust his bodymind to make the appropriate response to all environmental stimuli.

In the *Early Civilizing Stage*, the second stage in Alexander's theory, Man started to develop and use his ability to reason. The power of reasoning was used to master the desires of his instincts and senses in order to gain his ends, basically to control his external world. During this period, tools and shelters were developed and a process began which has continued to such dramatic effect to the present day; we have achieved a remarkable degree of control of the world about us, and have the tangible objects around us to prove it – television, cars, skyscrapers, etc. The problem, however, as Alexander saw it, was that while we were using our minds in what he called 'conscious control' to master the outside world we were not applying this same process to adapt our bodyminds to this new world we had created. We were missing out the 'T' in the vital I.T.O. sequence. He called this 'end-gaining'. The inevitable result was a physical deterioration and this, as Alexander clearly points out, had repercussions: 'because of the interrelation and interdependence of the mechanisms and potentialities of the organism in the process we call human life, any deterioration on the so-called physical side must, in time, seriously affect the so-called mental side'.[1]

The final stage in Alexander's theory, the *Later Civilizing Stage*, was when people grew aware of this physical decline and began to do something about it. This is where his theory of evolution ties up with his criticism of conventional exercise systems. This stage, incidentally, seems to have begun around the turn of the century.

The problem now was that Man, in his attempt to overcome his physical deterioration, adopted the approach that had been responsible for his decline in the first place. That is, in his haste to reach the goal (of remedying this physical state) he failed to attend to the *means-whereby* the goal was best achieved. Man was still end-gaining in his attempt to overcome a problem originally caused by his end-gaining habits.

What concerned Alexander in particular was the choice of

[1] E. Maisel *The Alexander Technique*

strength-building exercise systems. As he saw it, these systems failed to appreciate the basic principles of correct habits of Use upon which the Alexander Principle is based, and by means of which Man could halt this process of physical decline. In certain cases, not only did this muscle-building approach result in no improvement, but actually led to even worse habits.

Faulty Use leads to faulty posture and this fact enabled one of Alexander's pupils, Dr W. Barlow, actually to test these assertions. Dr Barlow made a number of measurements of a group of people, some of whom had faulty posture, who were given a series of conventional strengthening exercises. His findings at the end of the test period bore out Alexander's claim – the number of postural defects had increased.[1] No wonder, then, that Alexander teachers use the analogy of the rusty gate, which, when moved to and fro, doesn't loosen itself, it falls off.

Now, this is all very interesting, but how does it relate to golf? One answer concerns the correlation between end-gaining and the means-whereby principles to those golfing problems of 'head-up' and 'mind-wandering'. The other revolves around an explanation of exactly what is happening to our muscles during the performance of strength-building exercises. The latter will be considered first. Many of the exercises used by golfers are identical to those that were causing concern to Alexander. Calisthenic-type exercises, perhaps involving press-ups or weights, result in the repeated contractions of the muscles involved in the exercise. The danger is that this process, if overdone, can lead to a problem with serious implications for the golfer: '... overconcentration and shortening of anatomical muscle may result in the muscle spindle going silent, i.e. failing to feedback information to the brain about how the muscles are contracting.'[2]

The muscle spindle, incidentally, is the structure attached to the main muscle and to nerves which convey information to the brain. It is this information which amounts to what the golfer knows as 'feel' – an ingredient essential to successful golf. Clearly too much strength-building exercise can have a disastrous effect. Ben Hogan seems to have had an intuitive understanding of this process for he always refused to lift heavy bags before a tournament. This brief introduction to muscle physiology offers an interpretation of what may be happening to the golfer when he 'cracks-up' under pressure: his muscles have contracted because of the mental tension and he is just not getting the muscular feedback he needs.

[1] 'Report on Postural Deformity' *Proceedings of the Royal Society of Medicine* Vol. 49, No. 9, p. 670, 1950

[2] W. Barlow *The Alexander Principle*, p. 55

With regard to the first part of the answer, I must say that Alexander's work and particularly his chapter 'The Golfer who cannot keep his eyes on the ball' made very good reading. My besetting sin for two seasons was 'head-up'. I would go out to play with one thought in my mind – I had to keep my head down. The harder I tried the worse it became. A friend of mine used to do a take-off of my putting action in the club-house. My problem was one recognized by modern psychology, 'if the will puts itself in direct opposition to other psychological processes, such as imagination, emotions or drives, it will often be overpowered.'[1] My will-power was certainly overpowered!

Alexander understood the process well. His explanation of this failure of the will was that it was another example of the 'end-gaining' process. In Alexander's words it is 'the golfer's habit to work directly for his ends on the "trial and error" plan without giving due consideration to the means-whereby those ends should be gained'.[2] This implies a golfer interested only in the result of the shot or one who wants to hit a good shot but who is failing to think of the 'means-whereby' of hitting that shot.

The golfer seeking to cure this problem is immediately faced with another, for, as Alexander is quick to point out, learning the correct Use that would solve the problem is a matter of learning sensations that will at first feel strange. As he says, this Use is 'accompanied by certain sensory experiences (feelings) which, from their lifelong association ... have become very familiar' and 'from their very familiarity have come to "feel right"'. This is something that should be understood by the golf professional trying to get his pupil to adopt a new technique or method. The golfer may initially need to be shown clearly what is happening because his senses may be telling him something different.

In the wider perspective this mis-Use that has resulted in our physical and golfing problems can be seen as a symptom of the over-emphasis in our culture on achievement. The 'means-whereby' corresponds to the concept of awareness selected in the Introduction as a basic Systems quality.

I shall not outline here what is involved in learning the method of correct Use according to the Alexander Principle. This is not simply because it would be like trying to describe what it feels like to laugh or cry, but mainly because it is only satisfactorily taught by a trained leader in a one-to-one, teacher/pupil relationship, the aim

[1] R. Assagioli *The Act of Will*, p. 46
[2] F. M. Alexander *The Use of Self*

being 'to teach a pupil to associate a new sequence of thought with a new manner of using the body'.[1]

What is important, however, are the main concepts on which the Principle is based. In fact, the posture suggested in the 'Square-to-Square' method of contemporary golf theory is very similar to that of someone applying Alexander's methods. My Alexander teacher, on the few occasions that she played golf, was only able to make contact with the ball when she put her training into practice. So having digressed briefly, let us now return to the original discussion.

*In Favour of Exercises – Press Ups and Other Things*

While Alexander was an outspoken critic of strength-building exercises there are other golfers who adopt a different point of view. One of the great advocates of physical fitness and strength as an aid to golfing performance is Gary Player. At times the approach adopted by the man who once described himself as 'the fittest thirty-five year old in the world' appears to have bordered on the fanatical.[2] During one period of his life, Player claims to have spent a minimum of two hours a day strengthening his body. He was apparently capable of doing as many as one hundred press-ups at one go.

This approach seems to involve a mixture of calisthenic-type exercises as well as working with weights and grips of various shapes and sizes. The underlying philosophy is based on Player's own philosophy: 'I must keep driving myself forward, I just cannot be satisfied with anything less than the best in condition and performance of which I know I am capable.'[3]

What cannot be disputed is that in Player's case this approach has been enormously successful. Two points, however, must be made. Firstly, for those horrified at the thought of doing one hundred press-ups at a time, the Systems concept of equifinality does provide the reassurance that there are other ways of reaching your goal. Secondly, while obviously muscle building helps to hit the ball a long way which is crucial in the modern game, rhythm, timing and balance are just as important. The problem is that calisthenic-type exercise is indirectly related to these three factors. So if the exercises are to be used they must be followed by loosening and stretching

[1] W. Barlow *The Alexander Principle*, p. 173
[2] *Golf World*, November 1971
[3] *Golf World*, November 1971

exercises. No doubt Player is well aware of this but it does not always come across when his methods are mentioned.

SUMMARY

The solution to our dilemma appears to lie somewhere between these contradictory views; in the selection of an exercise system based on the 'means-whereby' principle and on the correct use of the bodymind. While Alexander does not seem to have come across any such system that met his approval, they do exist and will be considered at a later stage (Chapter 4). They tend, incidentally, to be the eastern systems which involve the mind in the performance of exercise.

## RECOMMENDED FURTHER READING

Books by Alexander are currently out of print, and anyway most people find them difficult reading. For further study, however, the following should be consulted:

1) W. Barlow *The Alexander Principle*
2) E. Maisel *The Alexander Technique*
3) F. Pierce Jones *Body Awareness in Action*

# *Chapter Four*

## THE MENTAL SIDE – SUGGESTED APPROACHES

*'You cannot play scratch golf, or better, till you are as full of confidence as an egg is full of meat.'*

*'Golf is played as muckle by the heid as by the hand.'*

One good reason why the mental side of golf has received so little attention, in spite of its widely recognized importance, was the state of development of the science of the mind, psychology. The enormously influential theories of Sigmund Freud brought an understanding of the manner in which our behaviour and motivation are determined by unconscious urges and anxieties and by the drives of the body. These insights led to the conclusion that we, as individuals, were not in a position to determine the course of our own lives; we were not in the driving seat.

However, most of Freud's work was based on observations of individuals who were psychologically the least healthy in society. The 'new' psychologies, on the other hand, base their studies on the 'healthiest' and what society might define as 'best'. This changed emphasis has revealed very different conclusions and a considerably more optimistic view of the position of the individual in society. It has led to the development of several psychologies which adopt what is basically a Systems approach: Ego psychology,[1] Bodymind psychology,[2] as well as the Psychology of Consciousness[3] and of the Will[4]

And it is with an understanding of the great potential of these developments that Timothy Gallwey can say:

[1] Psychocybernetics, autosuggestion, self hypnosis, etc.

[2] See Ken Dychtwald *Bodymind*

[3] In particular the work of Robert Ornstein and Charles Tart

[4] Roberto Assagioli and Rollo May are two of the major influences in this field.

'I believe that the great advances in athletic performance will come primarily not because of increased physical conditioning or better techniques, but because of advances in our abilities to concentrate our minds and free ourselves from mental limitations.'[1]

These developments also hint at steps that we ourselves can take to do something about Johnny Miller's conviction that 'we are presently using only ten percent of our brain's capabilities in golf'.[2]

What follows is a consideration of these 'new' fields with the aim of integrating them with those approaches which have already been suggested by various writers who sought to advise golfers. None of these suggested approaches, it should be said, evolved particularly with golf, or even sport, in mind. There is no doubt, however, as to their relevance.

## *Positive Thinking and the Self-Confidence Problem*

In any golf tournament there will, in a technical sense, be only one winner. If there are two hundred entrants for the tournament there will be one hundred and ninety-nine people who have, relatively, failed. How do these one hundred and ninety-nine people handle their failure? This vast majority potentially have self-confidence problems, and confidence as we all know, occupies a central place amongst matters which affect golfing performance. It is all too easy to let the failure lead to self-criticism and negative thoughts which, of course, is the step most likely to lead to yet another failure. The player soon becomes trapped within a downward spiral of negative thoughts – achieving the failure he constantly expects.

The recognition of this negative thought sequence led to the influential work of Norman Vincent Peale, Dale Carnegie and Dr George Hall. Amongst the golfing community, the best known 'positive thinker' is certainly Dr Peale – due to his influence on Gary Player who strongly recommends Peale's books and his views in *Gary Player, World Golfer*.

The argument underlying positive thinking was stated by the great philosopher-psychologist, William James, at the beginning of this century: 'The greatest discovery of my generation is that human beings can alter their lives by altering their attitudes of mind'.[3] Peale, Carnegie and Hall have all done good work in popularizing this concept whose relevance to the golfer is made quite clear by

[1] T. Gallwey *Inner Tennis*

[2] J. Miller *Pure Golf*

[3] Quoted in N. V. Peale *The Power of Positive Thinking*

Johnny Miller: 'You must remember that your golf swing will always be basically what it was when you first developed it in the early stages of your golf. Even after refining it and changing bits and pieces of it, if a guy hasn't seen you in ten years, since your amateur days, he could spot your swing from three fairways over ... ' Many people make mental changes, however, and that's the difference really between winners and non-winners.

The most immediate application of 'positive thinking' concerns the individual shots which make up the game. Adopting a positive mental approach means *visualizing* each shot before it is hit. The experts come out very strongly in favour of this. Jack Nicklaus even feels that having a positive image of the outcome of the shot before it is hit accounts for as much as fifty per cent of its eventual success.[1] Johnny Miller sees visualization as being the means-whereby we can begin to utilize the remaining ninety per cent of our mental faculties. We have to 'see ourselves' playing *pure golf* he concludes.[2]

Miller advocates using visualization for various other aspects of the game; planning the round, your golfing goals, your swing and even your overall game. He sees the brain as a computer with visualization as the programme that gets it working. Alex Morrison has suggested that these visualizations should and can be done while sitting comfortably at home.[3]

To complement these words of advice from expert golfers we have some clear evidence from the medical world. American physiologist, Edmund Jacobson, has shown that imagining a specific activity affects the muscles involved. Jacobson was able to measure contractions of muscles involved in running when his subjects imagined that particular activity.[4] Noted biochemist, Robert S. De Ropp, has also studied the technique and recommends it strongly in his excellent book *The Master Game* where he calls it *inner and outer theatre.*

Thus, the best answer to a lack of self-confidence is *positive visualization.* The difficulty, of course, is that it is easiest to do when your game is going well. Nevertheless, it is important to stick with it whether it seems to be working or not, applying it particularly when under pressure or in the crisis situation. It is such a powerful technique that one wonders what the effect of its widespread application would be.

It might help, by way of a conclusion, to keep in mind the following 'seed thoughts':

[1] J. Nicklaus *Golf My Way*

[2] J. Miller *Pure Golf*

[3] A. Morrison *Better Golf without Practice*

[4] Quoted in Samuels and Samuels, *Seeing with the Mind's Eye* pp. 66–176, and an excellent book on visualization techniques

> All we are is the result of what we have thought.
>
> *Dhammapada*

> What people visualize is what they get. Likewise what they have is the result of what they have visualized.
>
> *Samuels and Samuels*

*The Question of Goals*

The second approach applicable to the mental side of golf is Dr Maltz's self-image psychology, outlined in his book *Psychocybernetics.* Dr Maltz is a plastic surgeon who discovered that changing a man's face by surgery invariably changed the image he had of himself. This led to changes in behaviour, personality, and sometimes, argues Dr Maltz, even in his talents and abilities. This is because 'all your actions, feeling, behaviour ... are always consistent with this self-image.'[1]

For Dr Maltz the starting point is the projection of the positive self-image. He argues that positive thinking only really works to the extent that it is consistent with your self-image. In other words, your idle, positive thoughts of winning the British Open are of little use if the self-image only aspires to the Club Championship. To quote Systems Theory: progress must be 'within limits defined as reasonable'.[2]

Psychocybernetics is based on the newly emerging science of cybernetics, a science which studies the goal-oriented behaviour of machines.[3] This new science provides the reason why positive visualization is so important, as Dr Maltz points out:

> Cybernetics regards the human brain, nervous system and muscular system as a highly complex 'servo-mechanism' (an automatic goal-seeking machine which 'steers' its way to a target or goal by use of feedback data and stored information, automatically correcting course where necessary).[4]

Psychocybernetics gives the impression that once the bodymind is set a goal (i.e. by visualizing) it will be achieved almost without further effort. Dr Maltz repeatedly states that the goal is achieved *automatically,* describing the human system as a self-aiming torpedo

[1] Dr Maltz *Psychocybernetics,* p. 2
[2] F. E. Emery *Systems Thinking,* p. 10
[3] Systems Theory, incidentally, is the science which studies the goal orientated behaviour of living systems (see Chapter 9)
[4] Dr Maltz *Psychocybernetics,* p. 37

or missile[1] and implying that it is designed to cope with whatever problems or challenges are posed by the environment.[2]

There may well be some confusion here for what emerged from Alexander's work was a clear criticism of the end-gaining or goal-orientation that is being advocated so strongly by Dr Maltz. Alexander, like Dr Maltz, was acutely aware of the importance of ends or goals but was making two very important points. The first of these was that because of the state of inaccurate sensory appreciation of the human organism, the correct response to environmental stimuli was *not* automatic as it had been in the first stage of our evolution, the Uncivilized Stage, when man's state of sensory appreciation was highly developed.

The second point was that once the goal was set it was necessary to concentrate not on the goal but on the means-whereby that goal could be reached. The distinction is vital. When Tony Jacklin won the Open at Royal Lytham he was end-gaining in the sense that he wanted to win the Open but he understood fully how he needed to concentrate on the means-whereby if he was ever to achieve his goal. The means-whereby in his case was thinking of one shot at a time and not the implication of what he was doing. What is more, he was able to stick to the 'means' while under the greatest pressure.

In spite of these two weaknesses Dr Maltz's book has, like the Positive Thinkers, done useful work in drawing attention to the mental obstacles – negativity – that we so often place in our paths. And, as we shall see, the concept of goals is one that occupies a central place in the Systems approach to the golfing bodymind.

### *Psychosynthesis, Sub-Personalities and Self*

The next approach to be discussed – Roberto Assagioli's 'Psychosynthesis' – will be new to many golfers. This indicates that they have failed to follow up the recommended bibliography in Michael Murphy's *Golf in the Kingdom* which is a pity for there is much of relevance in this remarkable system of practical psychotherapy. What psychosynthesis does, is to develop further, within an integrated conceptual framework, many of the ideas and techniques that have already been introduced.

One of the most useful developments is the notion that we have not one but a number of different sub-selves or sub-personalities. Many of these little 'Is' will be fairly obvious: I am a father, I am a

[1] Ibid. p. 17
[2] Ibid. p. 30

businessman, I am a golfer, I am aggressive/placid, etc. Others will be less so, becoming apparent only after a certain amount of probing. Still others will not be apparent at all, being deeply embedded in the unconscious.

What is important for us is that the game of golf seems to involve these different aspects of ourselves, particularly those relating to the emotions. It also has a habit of involving those more troublesome, less desirable aspects of ourselves. As Shivas would say: 'nowhere does a man go so naked'.

The different sub-personalities can be put against each other by the various events that take place on the course so that they literally end up fighting each other. As each little 'I' is vested with amounts of energy the golfer is effectively wasting energy on internal conflict rather than channelling it all into the job in hand. An analogy sometimes used in psychosynthesis is that of an orchestra without a conductor and with all the instruments playing their own tune. Without a lead the individual, like the orchestra, also lacks direction and, in Assagioli's words, is 'tossed hither and thither by external influences', and as a result is 'often discontented, insecure and changeable in his moods thought and actions. Feeling intuitively that he is one, and yet finding he is divided unto himself.'[1]

It becomes clear that it is of vital importance to gain control of these different aspects of the personality; failure to do so will probably mean that we have more than the golf course to contend with. Our negative sub-personalities cannot be left behind once we arrive on the first tee; golf, as we have said, has a habit of stimulating them.

The first stage in acquiring control is to develop a thorough knowledge of these particular sub-personalities.[2] Psychosynthesis uses a number of different methods to accomplish this, even drawing from psychoanalysis to deal with the personalities hidden from the conscious mind. These techniques include guided imagery, dream analysis and simply talking about and writing down the characteristics of the particular sub-personality.

This 'awareness' stage is very important and will often involve probing into the darker sides of our being. We have a recognized

[1] Roberto Assagioli *Psychosynthesis*, p. 20

[2] One well-known technique for developing knowledge of sub-personalities which has become very popular in the U.S.A. is the Encounter Group, in which a safe environment is created to enable the participants to share their feelings about themselves and about the group. Other newly developed techniques involving work with the subconscious include bioenergetics, Rolfing (deep massage) and Dr Janov's controversial primal therapy.

tendency to suppress or attempt to disown those aspects we like least. This suppression, as Wilber points out, does not work; it is a 'gesture ... ultimately as futile as trying to deny our elbows' and it has two basic consequences:

> One, we no longer feel these aspects are ours, and so we can never use them, act upon them, satisfy them: our base of action is thus drastically narrowed, reduced and frustrated. Two, these facets now appear to exist in the environment – we have given our energy to others, and so that energy now seems to turn on us, to boomerang.

and further

> Our energy remains ours, but ... its source appears external to us, and so instead of possessing this energy we feel hammered by it, buffeted and slammed around by what now appears to be 'external' forces, so that we are driven mercilessly like a helpless puppet, with the environment *apparently* pulling the strings.'[1]

Wilber's words make it clear that suppression merely increases the problems that face us on the course. It makes the environment more hostile, and the mental control we are after even more difficult to attain.

Assuming the golfer has now successfully completed the first stage of his psychosynthesis, the next step is to gain control of the sub-personalities some of which will be new to the conscious mind. According to Dr Assagioli this is best achieved by *dis-identification:* 'We are dominated by everything with which our self becomes identified. We can dominate and control everything from which we dis-identify ourselves.'[2]

We need to learn to act and at the same time to be aware of our actions. It should be appreciated that the emotional dimensions of the personality that are often aroused on the golf course are very powerful. They are quite capable of taking us over. If, however, these emotions are viewed objectively they seem to lose their destructive force. The vested energies thus released can be used to more positive ends. On the golf course two sub-personalities which have destructive power are Mr Angry and Mr Anxious. Psychosynthesis suggests that we should observe them in action and perhaps confront them with a positive personality such as Mr Courage or Mr Determined.

Sometimes it may be genuinely difficult to reconcile two conflicting

1 Ken Wilber *The Spectrum of Consciousness*, p. 201
2 Roberto Assagioli *Psychosynthesis*, p. 22

sub-personalities. They may be totally incompatible. For example, the personality that wants to be a good golfer may be incompatible with the personality that wants to be a good husband or a good gardener. However, maintaining the position of observer makes the possibility of compromise more likely. Another solution is allocating time and space to each sub-personality in what is appropriately called, time-sharing. Failure to do this means that the sub-personalities are likely to be doing battle both on the golf course *and* at home *and* in the garden.

Dis-identification or de-tachment underlies the mental dimension of our Systems concept of awareness. It is the means-whereby of gaining conscious control. From this perspective we can say that while the Alexander Technique aims at conscious control largely through the physical body, psychosynthesis aims at the same end by integrating the mental processes.

### *The Emerging Self*

The practice of detachment from the multiplicity of selves leads on naturally to the third stage when the individual starts to become aware of his or her *true Self.* It is as if the Self only becomes evident once we come to see through all the little selves or sub-personalities. If, however, we make no attempt to discover our true Self it tends to remain hidden behind the confused and conflicting maze of sub-personalities.

This concept of the true Self is difficult but it is also of great importance. The true Self tends first to become apparent in the form of an image, a powerful image of what we ourselves can become. It is the internal vision of our true potential, our true capacity. The image is so powerful it seems to involve our entire mind and body and will tend to thrill, excite or to frighten us. This latter reaction might appear surprising but it is well known psychologically that we often shy away from images of our true potential, particularly if our predominant mode of thinking is negative. This image of the true Self will depend very much on the particular individual.

> For some it may be the ideal of the artist who realizes and expresses himself as the creator of beautiful forms, who makes art the most vital interest and the animating principle of his existence, pouring into it all his best energies. For others it may be the ideal of the seeker after Truth, the philosopher, the scientist. For yet others it is a more limited and personal ideal, that of the good father or mother.[1]

[1] R. Assagioli *Psychosynthesis*, p. 25

It could also be the ideal of the golfer expressing himself through his game, or of overcoming the sternest obstacles both external or internal, or of realizing an achievement or goal such as winning the Walker Cup.

The vital nature of this stage in psychosynthesis is made clear by the British tennis star, Virginia Wade, who has written an excellent article on the subject in the first *Quest* magazine. The article is entitled 'How I Won Wimbledon: The secret of greatness is deciding what you truly want'. Miss Wade stresses the vital importance of the discovery and knowledge of the true Self. She puts it like this: 'You can go an incredibly long way without that last ounce, but it's essential as the winning factor and also the hardest to put into the equation.'[1]

This awareness of the true Self is so 'essential' because it acts as a force which unites our many sub-personalities. It is the 'conductor of the orchestra' in our earlier analogy. This unity and harmony of the sub-personalities is the vital prerequisite of the transcendent performances on the sports fields; it seems to separate the real champions from the rest of the pack and to make them capable, sometimes, of those apparently superhuman feats so thrilling to us all.

What has emerged is this concept of the Self which can also be seen as the goal of the individual – to realize that potential which at this stage is only an image in the mind. Assagioli's psychosynthesis now starts to fit in with Dr Maltz's psychocybernetics with its emphasis on goal-orientation. These two approaches are also in harmony in recognizing the natural manner in which the individual tends to move himself towards that goal of self-realization, overcoming the obstacles that appear in the way. Assagioli, however, like Alexander, stresses the early steps that are necessary before this goal-orientation occurs automatically.

Once the true Self becomes apparent, even if circumstances knock the individual off course, the image of the Self will help him find his way back. This fits in with the Systems view which states, as we have said, 'that the basic regulation of the open system is self-regulation'. In the context of the Alexander Principle this was the state of affairs in the first stage of the theory of our evolution – the Uncivilized Stage – when the high quality of sensory appreciation of the bodymind served to guide us accurately in our daily life. Psychosynthesis adopts a more mental approach to isolate this 'unifying and controlling Principle of our life'.[2]

1 *Quest* magazine, 1978

2 R. Assagioli *Psychosynthesis*, p. 24

*Will-Power and Will in Golf*

There is a misconception amongst many golfers that will-power and effort is the key to success in golf. Psychologists know well that this is often not the case. In the last chapter I referred to the failure of my will-power to control my 'head-up' problem. Freud's theories explained that this was because of the powerful effect on the *unconscious*. As Rollo May points out:

> He [Freud] uncovered the vast areas in which motives and behaviour – whether in bringing up children or making love or running a business or planning a war – are determined by unconscious urges, anxieties, fears, and the endless host of bodily drives and instinctual forces.'[1]

The clear implication is that we, as individuals, are not in control, we are not the 'independent variable' and after a long spell of uncontrollable 'head-up' it was tempting to believe this early Freudian view of our basic nature. I, for one, was certainly not in control.

Psychosynthesis is able to provide a positive explanation in stressing the vital importance of integrating the unconscious aspects of the personality as a prerequisite to acquiring control. While will-power involves suppressing and forcing, the *will* operates in a very different way. 'A true act of will ... is an integral act which involves commitment of the whole person to a goal which is both realistic and worthwhile; such an act mobilizes energies of vast power.'[2] It is the will that is in action in directing the Self to its chosen goal in spite of the strong disruptive forces that will inevitably appear. The will is an act of unity and purpose that is only really possible once the true Self has begun to emerge. It is a decision which moves the individual towards the realization of that Self – an expression of total control, but as we have said it only functions after initial preparatory work.

SUMMARY

The approaches considered in this chapter have all stressed the importance of orientating the golfing bodymind in positive directions, towards positive goals. The more integrated of these,

[1] Rollo May *Love and Will*, p. 182

[2] Martha Crampton 'Psychological Energy Transformations: Developing Positive Polarisation' *Journal of Transpersonal Psychology*, No. 1, 1974

psychosynthesis, stressed the isolation and emergence of the true Self, which is the vital goal and task for us all. It also outlined effort or work necessary to hasten this emergence.

RECOMMENDED FURTHER READING

1) M. Maltz *Psychocybernetics*
2) R. Assagioli *Psychosynthesis*
3) R. Assagioli *The Act of Will*
4) Samuels and Samuels *Seeing with the Mind's Eye*
5) R. May *Love and Will*
6) J. Miller *Pure Golf*

SUBSIDIARY READING – on complementary approaches

7) Vernon Howard *The Power of Psycho-Pictography*
8) Ophiels *The Art and Practice of Getting Material Things through Creative Visualization*
9) William J. Ousby *Self Hypnosis and Scientific Self Suggestion*
10) Melvin Powers *Self-Hypnosis*
11) R. W. Wilde *Self-Improvement through Practical Psychology*
12) Leslie O. Korth *The Power of Auto-Suggestion*
13) A. D. Orage *Psychological Exercises and Essays*

# *Chapter Five*

## THE MIND/BODY SYNTHESIS

*'Here is a new commandment for you – Keep Your 'Mind's Eye' on the Ball.'*

*Regarding playing better in championships 'I put it down to concentration and confidence, with just a "sprinklin' o'carelessness" that keeps the muscles "soople" and the swing free and easy.'*

### *Yoga*

My first contact with the techniques of yoga was as a boy of seven or eight at a small seaside town some four hundred miles south of Calcutta, called Puri, site of one of the most famous Hindu shrines. Travelling entertainers were an integral part of Indian culture and the acts included dancing bears and monkeys and, of course, the snake charmer. On one occasion, a magic man called to entertain our family and one part of his repertoire, as I recall, was to open his mouth and show that it was empty. He then proceeded to put his hand in his mouth and pull out yards and yards of multi-coloured cloth. This, I later discovered, was a technique for internal cleansing used in yoga known as dhauti.

Stories like this, however, are more likely to discourage than anything else. One of the main problems is that many of the stranger yoga practices were devised for a culture in which they made practical sense. The cleansing technique described was a method of maintaining health in a hot climate with poor standards of hygiene.

In spite of certain misunderstandings, the techniques and methods that have been developed in India over thousands of years are becoming enormously popular in the western world; it is not surprising to hear that several of the world's leading golfers have taken to the discipline. Which type of yoga they practise is less clear for it should be appreciated that the subject matter is vast and there are many different forms of yoga. It is probably the postures and breathing techniques of Hatha yoga that have been practised. Hatha yoga, incidentally, is that branch of yoga which leads to mastery of the breath and control of the physical body.

Some of these postures and breathing practices are suggested as relevant to the golfing bodymind in a book available in America, *The Easy Way to Stay in Shape for Golf* by M. E. Deyo. This title is completely misleading. The Hatha yoga postures are *not* easy and gaining control of the physical body is *not* easy. In fact one of the translations of the Sanskirt word 'Hatha' is 'obstinacy', 'dogged perseverance' and 'stubborn will'. If you have these characteristics Hatha yoga is the branch of yoga most relevant for you. But while Mr Deyo's title is misleading, the rest of his book is certainly not.

This highlights a serious weakness in the approach of many golfers to their game: they spend their time searching for the easy way out and the miracle cure to their problems. This search is misguided for, in relation to the inner aspects of the game, progress is far from easy. Alexander puts it superbly when he says, 'Suppose you had the power to change a thief by magic, it would be of no use. The man would have had no experience in resisting temptation (that is, no experience of reacting rightly or wrongly to certain stimuli, and reacting ninety-nine times rightly to once wrongly) which is the experience a man must get before he can change from being a thief.'[1]

It is surely time to stop talking of 'easy ways'. The greatest satisfactions derive from the conquest of the hardest tasks. To help our game we need a demanding discipline – which yoga certainly provides. Success, in the words of the Indian philosopher Patanjali, is the result of 'tireless endeavour'.[2]

### *What Is Yoga?*

In the West, yoga is often associated with a series of difficult looking postures and complicated breathing techniques. It may, therefore, come as something of a surprise to hear that 'yoga is controlling the activities of the mind'.[3]

Nevertheless, this mental dimension is the direct result of a principle central to the practice of yoga: a fundamental mind/body

[1] E. Maisel *The Alexander Principle*, p. 8
[2] R. Assagioli *The Act of Will*, p. 235
[3] Pantanjali *Aphorisms of Yoga*, p. 25

unity. Control of the physical body is regarded as an essential prerequisite of mental control and therefore control of the breath is of particular importance as well, being seen as the function which unites our mental and physical processes.

This becomes apparent from a translation of the Sanskrit word 'yoga'. It is derived from the root 'yuj' which means to 'yoke' or 'join' and this refers not only to the mind and body but to the unity of the sub-personalities as well as unity of the individual with his true Self. Yoga thus has much in common with psychosynthesis. It understands fully that only by effecting an internal integration can the individual expect to function at full power. All yoga philosophy, all yoga techniques, are concerned with one thing – integration.

For the golfer, there is another matter of considerable interest. Yoga psychology makes a direct attack on anxiety which has been isolated as golfing problem number one by an eminent psychiatrist, in one of the very few books about the mental aspects of golf.[1] Anxiety is the very opposite of our Systems concept of equanimity but before entering a detailed discussion an introduction to the techniques of Hatha yoga is in order.

### *Yoga Postures*

In the earlier consideration of physical exercises used by golfers, such as calisthenics, it was suggested that while they may be of benefit in strengthening the muscles they could be detrimental in lessening the golfer's 'feel' for timing and balance. (See Chapter 3.) The conclusion was that the exercise system chosen by the golfer should be one that not only includes *all* the physical aspects, both strength and feel, but the mental aspects as well. There is no doubt that the techniques of Hatha yoga comprise just such a system, a means-whereby system. What is as important as each yoga posture is the mental effort that goes into its performance. Each individual posture or *asana* is a tremendous challenge and discipline for both mind and body. It is, therefore, of vital importance that you do not rush through the positions but perform each slowly and methodically.

In a wider context there is an altogether deeper meaning in the performance of yoga asanas. Central to yoga, and this is the tone of the whole human potential movement, is the idea that as individuals we operate at approximately ten to fifteen per cent of our true potential. What is more, our conception of our true potential is often

1 Dr David Morley *The Missing Links*

a considerable underestimation, which is basically what Positive Thinkers are saying. The object of yoga is to take the individual closer to the potential he conceives for himself and at the same time to revise his estimate towards his actual 'true potential'. The postures are an attempt to do this in a physical way, but as we have said the mind/body are so closely linked that any move towards our physical potential will be a move towards our mental potential.

What has now been introduced is the idea of the *edge* or boundary. This is very important, for if we are ever to reach our true potential we must learn about our 'edge' for it acts as a teacher. What is also important is that when we come close to our edge we must learn to move gently, for the edge is a sensitive area, largely uncharted and unknown and to move past it too quickly can be dangerous. Ken Dychtwald expressed this problem as follows:

> Physically, when I approach my edge gently and consciously, my body responds by focusing energy and attention on this spot, encouraging the blood and energy to bathe the related muscles and organs with vitality and life, thus allowing me the experience of true growth and self-nourishment. But if I do not try to reach my edge, my body, having no point of focus, will find it difficult to isolate the place and nourish it, and little growth and improvement will follow.
>
> To state the extremes: if I never explore my limits, my bodymind will gradually tighten and become unconscious. If I regularly explore my limits in a caring and adventuresome fashion, I will expand and grow. But if I try to push myself past where I am honestly able to go, I will no longer be practising 'yoga' but instead will be practising 'greed' and I will probably be met by pain and disease. Stated simply, it is the difference between ignoring yourself, making love to yourself, and raping yourself.[1]

The individual must thus move gradually towards his true potential, gently increasing his abilities and setting new, further limits. To try too much, too quickly would be too much of a strain. And so it is that a good yoga teacher will emphasize the difference between *stretching* and *straining* in the practice of postures. In this competitive world it is all too tempting to strain to keep up with those in front of you, or perhaps to opt out once you realize keeping up is not possible. Yoga teaches the balance between these two approaches.

[1] Ken Dychtwald *Bodymind*, pp. 66–7

*Yoga and Breathing*

All living systems, no matter how simple or complex, have one thing in common. They all take in energy from the environment, they transform the energy and then return some to the environment. In the human living system there are basically three of these vital *input – transformation – output* systems: the digestive-excretory process, the breathing process and the information process involving the mind and input/output via, in most cases, the senses. Of these three there seems to be little doubt that the one that receives the least attention is the breathing process. That, at least, is the case in the Western world. Elsewhere, however, the breath is seen as occupying a central role. Hazrat Inayast Khan of the Sufi tradition has stated that 'the subject of breath is the deepest of all the subjects ... breath is the most important thing in life.'[1] Breathing in yoga is seen as the function where the mind and the body unite ...

The particular relevance of breathing to the golfer is that it constitutes a means of controlling golfing enemy number one – anxiety. Simple observation of the breath will lead to an understanding of its intimate relationship with the emotions – a person crying or laughing is a good illustration. While the particular emotion is in itself extremely difficult to control, the breathing process is more tangible and thus more susceptible to control. So when anxiety leads to quick, shallow breathing, learning to slow and deepen will have a correspondingly calming effect. This is an example of achieving an end (equanimity) by attending to the means-whereby principle. The end-gainers reaction to anxiety is to worry which, of course, merely compounds the problem.

This quieting of emotion by concentrating on and controlling the breathing process works partly for physiological reasons but also because the attention is taken from the object of concern (usually failure) to something more mundane. It brings the thoughts from the future or the past right into the present.

There is another important aspect of breathing which should be considered. This lies in the very important similarity between a golf shot and a breath. Each breath that we take can be completely unnoticed or it can, when we turn our attention to it, come under our control. It has both a voluntary and an involuntary dimension, and as Murphy reminds us 'Every shot has a conscious component and an unconscious one, a voluntary control and one that is involuntary. To know how to strike the balance is the very essence of

[1] Quoted in Rama, Ballentine and Ajaya, *Yoga and Psychotherapy*, pp. 32–3

golfing skill.'[1] The golfer in the Western world tends to over-use his conscious component in relation to the shot and under-use it in relation to the breath. Murphy tells us we must learn to 'strike the balance' for to do so is to have the mind and body working together.

### *Concentration: Calming the Restless Mind*

If the mind is left completely to its own devices it has a habit of flitting from thought to thought in a random, largely haphazard manner. And if allowed to operate continuously in this undisciplined way, it tends to become easily distracted, unable to concentrate. This leads to a state of confusion and unease. Yoga aims to stop this 'flitting' and to bring this 'mind' under control. Those methods which employ both the body and the breath have been briefly considered. Let us now consider the path of *concentration* which is to be practised once the aspirant has mastered the control of the breath.

The yoga practice of concentration involves fixing the attention on a specific object and repeatedly returning it to the object when it has wandered. At first the person will find his mind shooting off all the time and will think that concentration is impossible. However, with regular practice the ability to concentrate and to intercept the wandering thoughts soon develops, until the mind centres without distraction on the object of concentration.

The value of the 'still' mind will have perhaps become apparent as a great asset to the top sportsman: Arthur Ashe, for example, was seen in the 1975 Wimbledon Final with his eyes shut, calming the mind. Ashe, it will be recalled, recorded a surprising, but nevertheless convincing, win over Jimmy Connors. This process of calming the mind is one method of isolating the true Self that was discussed at some length in the previous chapter. It will be considered again.

### *Yoga Psychology, Golf and the Concept of Attachment*

It is now relevant to consider and discuss what is seen in yoga psychology as the underlying cause of our anxiety and tension – and so considered to be of the greatest importance.

The cause of anxiety, according to yoga psychology is *attachment*; we become attached to objects, to images of ourselves, to thought patterns, to our habits and even to our neuroses. Yoga psychology

[1] M. Murphy *Golf in the Kingdom*, p. 194

points out that if the individual wishes to rid himself of anxiety he must rid himself of his attachments, he must let them go. For the golfer the first attachment to tackle is the one that we have to the image of ourselves as a failure. This was also the point made by positive thinking and psychocybernetics.

Following the thought through, however, we should eventually let go of even our positive thoughts and positive self-images. This is because even positive self-images can be a cause of anxiety when we see them being threatened as they undoubtedly will be in the competitive golfing arena. There are some interesting insights regarding this in Zen Buddhism which will be considered in the next chapter.

There is another aspect of this concept of attachment which is relevant. Attachment, it is said in yoga, results from the experience of pleasure; in golf, for example, the pleasure of a victory. What the pleasure is does not matter, but what is important is that it tends to lead to a *dependence* on that source, even though the source no longer gives us pleasure. This dependence has two important implications for the golfer. One is that it contradicts the Systems emphasis on being the independent variable in the relationship with the environment. The second point is that anxiety will result if that source no longer continues to gives us pleasure. Clearly, to be attached to something as ephemeral as a victory on the golf course is likely to act merely as an important source of anxiety and tension.

This is really another way of looking at Alexander's basic concepts and his criticism of end-gaining. Yoga points to the weakness of attachment to the 'end' and makes one very significant observation. This is that very closely related to attachment to 'ends' is the concept of *aversion.* Indeed, in yoga psychology aversion and attachment are seen as being two sides of the same coin. This implies that the very attachment to the goal of victory is what will lead to an aversion from the actual realization or attainment of that victory. The tendency of positive self-images to switch to negative self-images when the pressure builds up is a practical example of attachment switching to aversion.

The real problem with our attachments is that they are to things of a temporary nature: the victory fades into the past, material possessions waste away or lose their value. They are all here today, gone tomorrow. To attain equanimity we must look for that which is permanent, and this, according to the wise men of the East, is that truth that lies within, the truth of the inner Self. For them, this *is* the only truth worth pursuing.

There is, of course, no reason why the game of golf cannot be a means of carrying on this search. The game then becomes a quest to discover your inner nature. And from this viewpoint the victory is a case not only of contacting that inner Self but of giving expression to it through the medium of the game; an expression that involves the commitment of the mind, body and soul. Golf then becomes a dynamic art form. It is the game Shivas Irons would have us play. It is also, I suspect, somewhat akin to the game played by those who have produced truly great performances under pressure. They seem to have won a battle with themselves. It is a game, too, that we can all play – *the inner game of golf.*

SUMMARY

The most significant aspect of this chapter is that the vital mind/body interrelationship proposed by yoga provides the means of controlling the problem of tension or anxiety on the golf course. The body and the breathing process were shown to be good ways of reducing anxiety; concentrating the thoughts was shown to have the same effect. The final section brought these arguments together within the psychological observations on which yoga is based.

RECOMMENDED FURTHER READING

1) M. Murphy *Golf in the Kingdom*
2) M. E. Deyo *The Easy Way to Stay in Shape for Golf*
3) Rama, Ballantine and Ajaya *Yoga and Psychotherapy*
4) Theos Bernard *Hatha Yoga*
5) Lawrence Le Shan *How to Meditate: A Guide to Self Discovery*

For people unfamiliar with Hatha yoga postures and breathing two very good introductory books are:

6) Van Lysbeth *Yoga Self-Taught*
7) Yesudian and Haich *Yoga and Health*

# *Chapter Six*

# ZEN INSIGHTS

> Of Vardon *'He proves, as no other man does that golf is an art. I am sure the game is a pure joy to him; he makes every shot in such an effortless way.'*

The connection between Zen Buddhism and sport was first suggested some thirty years ago in Eugen Herrigel's charming book *Zen in the Art of Archery.* More recently the basic zen concepts have been applied successfully to tennis by Timothy Gallwey and to golf by Michael Murphy. These concepts tend to overlap with those developed in the last chapter, because both yoga and zen adopt a holistic Systems approach to life and its various problems.

## *Thinking and Not Thinking in Golf*

There is an apparent inconsistency amongst sports theories. Western writers are usually at pains to stress the value of positive thinking and, more appropriately, positive imaging. Eastern theorists on the other hand emphasize *not* thinking, introducing concepts such as Beginners Mind, Childlikeness and Non-Judgemental Awareness. Any thinking at all interferes with the natural 'doing' activities of the golfing bodymind. This point has occasionally been made by Western writers. Some fifty years ago Andra Kirkaldy made the following statement:

> How often – how very often have you driven a fine long ball just at that moment when you were thinking nothing at all about the way you drive it. That is what we are all aiming at – automatic golf. You have tried to repeat that drive, remembering how easily the ball left the club, so that you hardly felt the shot. But the very effort at repeating it spoilt it.

> You had become too self-conscious, and if you analyse your mind, it will be found that you have no faith in your ability to do it again.[1]

The words are pure zen and indeed could well come from one of the zen masters. Suzuki, for example, makes the same point: 'Man is a thinking reed but his great works are done when he is not calculating or thinking.'[2]

Most golfers will recognize the wisdom in these words and indeed will have experienced just what Kirkaldy is talking about. We tend, however, to think that the experience is something that just happens and realize that the very attempts to recreate it prevent the repetition. What the golfer *can* do is to take steps to make such moments of 'automatic golf' more likely to occur and perhaps after years and years of training actually develop the ability to create them at will. Herrigel's book outlines just such a training. He discusses at some length the strict, highly disciplined and often extremely frustrating training he followed while training in the zen art of archery.

### *Different Levels*

Before discussing in some greater detail certain aspects of this 'zen training' it is relevant to consider the different levels that have emerged in the context of these 'inner aspects' of the game of golf. These levels are important. They provide a means of reconciling the fact that having earlier suggested approaches that stressed 'positive *thinking*', we are now recommending zen and '*not thinking*'.

It should be remembered that the golfer is not confined to staying at one particular stage all the time and he will find that different methods and techniques become appropriate as he moves forward. Up to now, four distinct levels have emerged which may be said to represent four possible points from which to play the inner game of golf:

LEVEL I This level is characterized by a failure to understand, either cognitively or intuitively the inner aspects of the game of golf. The result is a golfer who tends not to be in control either of himself or his game and who tends to be tossed hither and yon by the vagaries of the game, looking outside for solutions to golfing problems and blaming all and sundry for golfing misfortunes. Other characteristics include a tendency to tension and anxiety, to emotional

[1] Andra Kirkaldy *My 50 Years of Golf – Memoirs*

[2] D. T. Suzuki in the introduction to *Zen in the Art of Archery* by Eugen Herrigel

fluctuation and an inability to concentrate. This golfer is also likely to be unable to remain in control when the pressure builds up in a tournament. This level can be called the *No Game Level,* i.e. no 'inner' game.

LEVEL II This level sees the emergence of an appreciation of the relevance of the inner game of golf and, more important, an attempt to do something about it. This willingness or receptiveness is significant because the desire to change must come from within if it is ever to be effective. The golfer is now beginning to accept full responsibility for his actions on the golf course.

Techniques such as positive thinking, psychocybernetics and, particularly, visualization begin to be applied and experimented with. The earlier insights from psychosynthesis suggest the importance of the knowledge and integration of the many sub-personalities, involving the exploration of both conscious and unconscious. This level can be called the *Ego level.*

LEVEL III Having begun to think in positive rather than negative terms and more in images than thoughts, the golfer may begin to appreciate the need to integrate the body with the mind. Now the techniques of Hatha yoga come into their own with their emphasis on body awareness (Alexander's sensory appreciation), relaxation through the body and through breathing, and on detachment.

Detachment, it will be recalled, is the means to knowledge of sub-personalities and of the true Self. This level is, in fact, characterized by the recognition of the importance of the knowledge of this true Self and by the searching that precedes its appearance.

This level is the *Existential level.*[1] While the Ego level was concerned with the awareness of the mind, this level involves the awareness of both mind *and* body and of the feelings behind the thoughts.

LEVEL IV The final level involves breaking down that which Levels II and III have been working to build. The individual is now beginning to realize the limitations of the individual Ego and seeks to go beyond, he is seeking to return to the first stage, in Alexander's theory of evolution, when he need no longer exert 'conscious control' and can trust the responses of the bodymind. He has developed his sensory appreciation to such an extent he can switch 'off' or at least switch 'on' to automatic.

This level is based on an assumption:

> The assumption is that we can, and indeed must, trust our biological nature in order to allow the evolution of our highest

[1] See Ken Wilber's *The Spectrum of Consciousness* for an excellent analysis of these different levels or, as he calls them, 'wave lengths' of consciousness.

> potentials. The passive quality associated with allowing implies that there is within us a source of wisdom which transcends the conscious ego.[1]

We can call this level the *Zen level.* It involves moving beyond the golfing mind and body and into the unknown. It is important that these steps into the beyond are only taken when the golfer is ready. As Shivas warns 'Ye must have a solid place to swing from, before ye open up so wide, otherwise ye'll be swept away.'[2]

Integrating up to Level III must precede work towards Level IV.

### *Certain Characteristics of Working towards the 'Zen' Level*

The zen level involves certain new ideas and concepts which are likely to be unfamiliar; they are involved in the zen training undertaken by Eugen Herrigel.

#### BEGINNER'S MIND

One of the central notions in zen is that we must become what we once were; to return, it seems, from whence we came. 'Childlikeness', Suzuki tells us, 'has to be restored after long years of self-forgetfulness.'[3] And Herrigel, in talking of the Japanese swordmaster, makes the same point:

> The swordmaster is as unselfconscious as the beginner. The nonchalance which he forfeited at the beginning of his instruction he wins back again as an indestructable characteristic. But, unlike the beginner, he holds himself in reserve, is quiet and unassuming, without the least desire to show off.[3]

This is like the young golfer new to the game who putts like a demon and seemingly without fear. Yet as he grows old he seems to lose this skill. Zen Buddhism works to recover this 'Beginner's Mind'.

In the golfing context, Beginner's Mind is a mental freshness, an approach to each round as if it were the first round you had ever played. Former British and American Open Champion, Tony Jacklin recognizes this when he writes:

[1] Frances Vaughan Clark in *Journal of Transpersonal Psychology*, No. 93 (1974)
[2] M. Murphy *Golf in the Kingdom*, p. 190
[3] Herrigel *Zen in the Art of Archery*

> With a fresh, clear mind and outlook, which I think are so important, inspiration comes out far more naturally, and we then allow our true talent to come out.

And speaking of Jack Nicklaus:

> One of the key factors in his career ... much more than he is given credit for is his mental outlook, his fresh mental outlook.[1]

NON-JUDGEMENTAL AWARENESS

We have an opportunity both to teach ourselves Beginner's Mind, and to benefit from it every time we hit a shot. We can do this if we stop ourselves evaluating every shot. These evaluations just set the thinking mind working again and the thoughts tend, in most golfers, to become negative. Golfers often make an implied judgement by looking away in disgust from the bad shot. This was something Shivas warned against, insisting 'that we follow the flight of every shot to the very end – no matter how bad that shot may be' and that 'we blind ourselves by turning away too soon'.[2] If we watch our bad shots we can learn from them, we learn little or nothing if we look away. If we don't judge we are less likely to miss that crucial sensory feedback that can tell us why we 'did wrong' and what we 'did wrong'.

LETTING GO

In the last chapter the emphasis in yoga psychology on 'non-attachment' was stressed. In zen the same concept is introduced in terms of 'letting go'. This means particularly the letting go of that which inhibits us from reaching our potential – the ego-thinking mind, which is concerned with ends or goals whereas the whole emphasis in zen is on the Means. Zen thus stresses non-doing, non-striving or what Fred Rohe calls the 'progress-by-less' method.[3]

Timothy Gallwey, a teacher of the inner game of tennis, teaches his pupils not to try to hit the ball. This is very different from either trying to hit it or trying to miss it. It is the zen approach. As he so rightly points out, the supreme irony of the 'inner game' is that you gain control as you let go; success follows the abandonment of the wish to succeed.

SUMMARY

The zen approach to sport is radical in that it challenges so

[1] *Golf Monthly*, March 1978

[2] M. Murphy *Golf in the Kingdom*, p. 179

[3] Fred Rohe *The Zen of Running*

fundamentally many of the notions that underlie the Western approach – the emphasis on effort and achievement in particular. What is exciting about zen is that it directs itself to the state of mind that characterizes the attainment of potential. One important point was emphasized: work is necessary (on Levels II and III) before the individual can proceed with safety towards the peaks. The more Western approaches tend to concentrate on these earlier levels. All are relevant, but in their own time.

## RECOMMENDED FURTHER READING

1) Eugen Herrigel *Zen in the Art of Archery*
2) Michael Murphy *Golf in the Kingdom*
3) Timothy Gallwey *The Inner Game of Tennis*
4) Timothy Gallwey *Inner Tennis*
5) Robert E. Ornstein *The Psychology of Consciousness*
6) Robert E. Ornstein *The Nature of Human Consciousness*
7) D. T. Suzuki *Zen Mind, Beginners Mind*

# *Chapter Seven*

## THE SYSTEMS SYNTHESIS

*'I feel after reading books that my golf becomes a mixture of Vardon here, Taylor there, Braid somewhere else and myself nowhere.'*

*Bringing It All Together*

Teachers of golf technique sometimes tell their pupils that they should acquire and perfect a method which will stand up under pressure. This is indeed a valid point for there is no doubt that extensive practice of a sound method will go a long way to ensuring that the swing stays with the golfer regardless of what is in his mind. The argument, however, does seem to imply that there is little else the golfer can do to survive the pressure.

I hope that the previous chapters have suggested that this is very far from being the case. The various techniques discussed provide insight into how the golfer can build his inner resources to enable him to stand alone when the time comes. There is another possible reaction to the pressure – the exciting possibility that the game's toughest competitive moments can act as the catalyst required to actually bring it all together to unify the golfing bodymind. It is a state of mind hinted at by the poet Yeats:

> When ... a man is fighting mad,
> Something drops from eyes long blind,
> He completes his partial mind.

Colin Wilson also suggests that 'when a man is galvanised by some crisis or ecstacy, the full moon suddenly appears, and he feels in control of his real powers'.[1]

In the golfing world the potential of this 'full moon' state has been

[1] C. Wilson *New Pathways to Psychology*, p. 243

excellently demonstrated by Tony Jacklin. Playing in the Lancôme Trophy in France, Jacklin dropped a stroke on the sixteenth hole in the final round. This produced a feeling of fear but it appeared to 'complete his partial mind' for he went into one of his invincible 'cocoons of concentration', and in his words,

> Everything came into focus. Although I could feel my club at every half-inch of my swing, I was free from thinking about various parts of my game. I hit my drive three hundred and fifty yards, about fifty yards farther than I had ever hit a ball in my life. The only way I could get to the hole was by hitting a four-iron as hard as I could and as high as I could which was ridiculous, really, because this was a long par-five hole. I stood there with the four-iron and smashed it. I looked up and it was flying high and dead straight where I thought, six feet from the flagstick. I holed the putt for an eagle.[1]

The birdie on the eighteenth was easy and Arnold Palmer was beaten by a shot. Jacklin was in control of his 'real powers'.

Not only did this experience of Jacklin's produce an incredible finish to the tournament but it shows superbly what it really means to 'get it all together', to get all the parts working as one. The whole really is something more than the sum of its parts.

So when you hear a description of golfers being in a 'world of their own' or playing golf 'on another level' it could indeed be true. There is no doubt that it is possible to play golf in a state of mind somewhat different from that which we normally experience. To reiterate the much quoted words of the philosopher/psychologist William James:

> Our normal waking consciousness is but one special type of consciousness, while all about it parted from it by the filmiest of screens there lies potential forms of consciousness entirely different. We may go through life without suspecting their existence but apply the requisite stimulus and, at a touch, they are there in all their completeness.

### *Altered States in Other Sports*

What is significant is that the sporting 'altered state of consciousness' (A.S.C.) is by no means as uncommon as one might suppose. Michael Murphy, for example, has collected a large number of

[1] Quoted in G. Leonard *The Ultimate Athlete*, p. 47

reports from leading sportsmen since *Golf in the Kingdom* was published.[1]

Also, in a programme produced by the BBC, a number of leading sportsmen talked of remarkable experiences. Racing driver Jackie Stewart, like Tony Jacklin, spoke of an incredibly heightened state of awareness during performance. He described a very strong scent of sweet smelling grass coming to him during a race which he likened to being in a 'long elongated cloud of freshly-cut grass'. Someone had run off the road while rounding a corner but Stewart's senses were so super-aware that he got this powerful smell which stayed with him for several minutes in spite of his going at such a high speed. Elsewhere, he speaks of time slowing down during a race so he was able to make manoeuvres that would normally have been impossible.[2]

Ian Thompson talked of running into the stadium when he won the marathon title in the 1974 Commonwealth Games. As he ran into the tunnel everything became totally quiet and, momentarily, he had a feeling of being outside himself. Another athlete, Roger Bannister, in *First Four Minutes,* writes of a day in Scotland some three years before his historic run:

> One day I had been swimming, and to get warm I started running. Soon I was running across the moor to a distant part of the coast of Kintyre. It was near evening and fiery sun clouds were chasing over to Arran. It began to rain and the sun shining brightly behind me cast a rainbow ahead. It gave me the feeling that I was cradled in the rainbow arc as I ran ... I felt I was running back to all the primitive joy that my season had destroyed ... I started to run again with the sun in my eyes nearly blinding me. I could barely distinguish slippery rocks from heathery turf or bog, yet my feet did not slip or grow weary now – they had new life and confidence. I ran in a frenzy of speed, drawn on by unseen force. The sun sank, setting the forest ablaze, and turning the sky to dull smoke. Then tiredness came on and my bleeding feet tripped me. I rolled down a heathery topped bank and lay there happily exhausted.[3]

Returning to the TV programme, hurdler David Hemery described his Olympic victory in a world record time for the 400 metre hurdles. During the race he felt he was an extension of his

[1] Now reported in a book by M. Murphy and Rhea White *The Psychic Side of Sport*

[2] M. Murphy 'Sport as Yoga' *Journal of Humanistic Psychology*, Vol 17, No 4, 1977

[3] Roger Bannister *First Four Minutes*, pp. 134-5

own thinking and that if he was going to fly over the hurdles that was the way it would be. Mike Brearley, England's cricket captain, spoke of such 'total absorption' that the bowling and his batting became part of the same thing.

Kenneth Ravizza, when researching sporting peak states of consciousness, interviewed two skiers who described experiences similar to Brearley's: 'I was really blending into the snow, the mountain ... I wasn't different from the hill. The whole environment was a part of me.' And the second skier reported:

> Everything was so perfect, everything so right, that it couldn't be any other way. The closest thing I can say about it was that there seemed to be tracks in the snow that my skis were made to fit in ... It was no longer me and the hill, but both of us, it was just right, for I belonged there.[1]

No doubt in the future many more sportsmen will come forward to tell their particular story. Perhaps the sports journalists will begin to report more than just the results!

## *The Systems Approach*

Until now few, if any, sportsmen have actually seen their sport as a means of experiencing peak states of consciousness, and fewer still have worked intentionally toward such an end. The experiences have just come upon them, as it were.

This was certainly the case with Tony Jacklin's experience. And while these moments have occurred some ten times in his career, he is fully aware that they are not something which can be created easily or at will: 'It comes and it goes, and the pure fact that you go out on the first tee of a tournament and say, "I must concentrate today" is no good. It won't work. It has to be there already.'[2] This vital point highlights the entire basis of the Systems approach to the golfing bodymind: to bring together the various approaches and techniques and make sure that *it* is 'there already'.

What the golfer must realize is that *it* will almost certainly not be there unless he has taken steps and done some work, piecing the parts together to prepare his golfing bodymind. The partial,

[1] Kenneth Ravizza 'Peak Experiences in Sport' *Journal of Humanistic Psychology* Vol 17, No 4 (1977)

[2] Dudley Doust 'Opening the Mystical Door of Perception in Sport' *The Sunday Times* 4 Nov. 1973

mechanistic, perfect technique approaches to golf must be combined with the holistic, Systems approaches to the game. The two approaches must be seen as complementary.

It is proposed to mention one final point which is somewhat ironic. There is no doubt that in terms of the individual golfing bodymind the potential for attaining this state of wholeness is enormous. When talking about his 'cocoon of concentration', Jacklin says, 'If I can put myself into that cocoon, I'm invincible.' There are many of us who would like to be invincible at golf, but our reasons are more likely to be related to the ego mind.

The thoughts of the golfer at the Ego level mentioned in the last chapter tend to revolve around success and failure. The motivational force of these thoughts is strong. Indeed Western culture is oriented towards the concept of success and this tends to be internalized in the individual. We all want to win, to be invincible. The irony is that the states of consciousness in which the individual is so totally in control that he feels invincible are characteristic of the Zen level, the level that moves beyond the thoughts of success or failure, the No Mind or Beginner's Mind. We must let go of all thoughts and trust our 'biological nature'.

SUMMARY

Systems theory looks at the whole rather than the parts. This chapter has discussed just what this state of 'wholeness' might mean on the golf course: a state of mind completely different from that of our daily lives, a state of control in which the whole is considerably greater than the sum of its parts. This could be called a condition of *Synergy*.

RECOMMENDED FURTHER READING

1) G. Leonard *The Ultimate Athlete*
2) C. Wilson *New Pathways in Psychology*
3) Lawrence Le Shan *How to Meditate*
4) A. M. Maslow *Towards a Psychology of Being*
5) C. Tart *Altered States of Consciousness*
6) C. Tart *States of Consciousness*
7) Robert E. Ornstein *The Nature of Human Consciousness*
8) Kenneth Ravizza 'Peak Experiences in Sport' *Journal of Humanistic Psychology* Vol 17, No 4. 1977

# *Part Two*

# THE SYSTEMS APPROACH

# *Chapter Eight*

## THE SYSTEMS APPROACH TO GOLF

*'I am thoroughly convinced that thousands of golfers today have had their game hopelessly ruined by neglecting simple first principles.'*

In the BBC's recent series 'The Long Search' one of the programmes contained an interview with the Berkeley physicist, Dr Fritjof Capra, who talked of the methods of classical, Newtonian physics. Dr Capra described the nature and methodology of the Newtonian approach to science. This was to dissect the system under observation. If this failed to produce an answer the dissections were broken down still further. This is typical of the approach which was adopted in other academic subjects:

> Classical science in its diverse disciplines, be it chemistry, biology, psychology, or the social sciences, tried to isolate the elements of the universe – chemical compounds and enzymes, cells, elementary sensations, freely competing individuals, as the case may be – expecting that by putting them together again conceptually or experimentally, the whole or system – cell, mind, society – would result and be intelligible.[1]

It is interesting that the conventional approach to golfing problems is classical or Newtonian. In order to understand the golf swing, it is dissected. The golf theorist, like the economist or the natural scientist, assumes other variables in the environment to be stable while studying in detail one particular part of the whole.

There is no doubt that the classical approach has had its successes. It is largely responsible for the great wealth of knowledge and understanding we now have as well as the sophisticated technology that provides many of the conveniences of modern life. In golf it has

[1] Ludwig von Bertalanffy in the Foreword of *Introduction to Systems Philosophy*, E. Laszlo

resulted in some two thousand books and numerous articles, all of which, in one way or another, have advanced the theoretical side of the game. But partial analysis does not tell the whole story. The scientists found, for example, that the supposedly 'stable' variables were less stable than they had initially thought, or that when combined together took on a different character, displaying synergistic/holistic properties which they could not afford to ignore.

To overcome these weaknesses in the classical approach, scientists have begun to study systems – from simple bacteria to complex modern business organization – as a whole and as open systems, dependent for their survival on the interactions with their particular environment. They are now studying interrelationships as well as the individual elements.

This approach is the domain of what its founder, Ludwig von Bertalanffy, has called 'General Systems Theory', or, as in this book, the Systems approach. In spite of being so new, the Systems approach has already had a dramatic influence in several major disciplines. The revolution in physics, with the resulting atomic and quantum theories of modern physics is possibly the most obvious example.

In the medical world, doctors are beginning to appreciate more fully the vital interactions of mind and body, as well as the emotional dimension of many illnesses. There is growing interest in psychosomatic and preventative medicine and the natural healing systems of traditional medicine, such as acupuncture and herbal cures. The World Health Organization, for example, now gives official backing to methods of traditional African witch doctors, while the over-readiness of Western doctors to prescribe pills is being criticized because it often merely treats the symptoms and not the cause. Like the traditional approach to golf, if the real cause is not diagnosed, the prescribed solution will often lead to other more complex problems.

In psychology, the development of humanistic and transpersonal psychology as well as the growing interest in the holistic Eastern psychologies of yoga and zen reflect the same trend. In my own discipline, management studies, Systems Theory has made its impact and, last but not least, the approach has resulted in new sciences such as ecology and cybernetics. Its pedigree is clearly excellent.

One of the main advantages of the Systems approach is that it provides a framework for re-interpreting the theories derived from partial analysis. In Chapter 2 conventional golf theory was regarded in this way. However, according to Emery 'there have ... been two arguments for a systems approach to the analysis of living phenomena.'[1] In this section of the book these two arguments have been adopted and provide the conceptual framework for an introduction to the Systems approach to the golfing bodymind.

The first of these arguments is that only such a holistic approach to the 'living system' will reveal its higher properties, characteristics and aspirations.

These properties can be isolated by posing again the question: what are the qualities/properties 'that enable the system to survive and adapt in its typical environment?'[2] The defined environment in our case was that of the top quality tournament golfer and the qualities isolated as a result of asking the question were those of concentration, equanimity and awareness. These vital qualities will be dealt with in this section.

The second argument is that there are certain characteristics common to *all* systems no matter how simple or complex and studying these will 'provide a valid and powerful form of generalization'.[3]

The first and, in our case, most important of these common characteristics is that of the 'goal-orientated' behaviour of all living systems. The chapter on goals (Chapter 9) discusses this vital question of motivation – aided by the work of psychologist Abraham Maslow, whose writing, retrospectively, would seem to follow a 'Systems' approach.

Chapter 13 discusses the relationship and relevance of the 'common characteristics' to the golfing bodymind. First we must establish whether the most basic aspects of 'the system' are operating smoothly. The 'common characteristics' argument can be applied with benefit to conventional golf theory. Jack Nicklaus, in fact, is a great advocate of 'getting the basics right' when talking of golfing technique. In our case the argument is applied rather differently.

The final chapter in this section considers some recent attempts to draw parallels between golf and religion. While this may not be for everyone and can certainly be omitted, it would seem to offer an interesting and exciting new dimension to this game of ours.

[1] F. E. Emery *Systems Thinking*, p. 7
[2] Ibid. p. 8
[3] Ibid. p. 7

## RECOMMENDED FURTHER READING

The most readable introduction to the Systems Approach I have come across is:

1) E. Laszlo *The Systems View of the World*

The interested reader might also like to consult:

2) E. Laszlo *Introduction to Systems Philosophy: Toward a New Paradigm of Contemporary Thought*
3) F. E. Emery *Systems Thinking*
4) L. von Bertalanffy *General Systems Theory*

# *Chapter Nine*

## THE COMMON CHARACTERISTICS ARGUMENT I

*'He [Mr Balfour] always seemed to play golf for the good he got out of it, and his form was for that very reason most consistent.'*

*Goals and Motivation*

As we have seen one of the distinctive characterics of living systems is the goal-directedness of their activities.[1] This point has been stressed by the Positive Thinkers, by Maltz's psychocybernetics, by Assagioli's psychosynthesis and by Systems Theory. It is clearly a matter of central importance to any living system, the golfer being no exception.

*Systems Theory and Goals*

An open system (in this case, the golfer) can only achieve a steady state (equanimity) when two conditions are fulfilled.[2] These are: (a) Unidirectionality. This means that whatever happens to the environment, the system remains oriented towards the same end. (b) With respect to that end, the system maintains a *rate of progress* towards it, within limits defined as tolerable.[3]

In relation to condition (a) it is relevant to recall the earlier discussion of psychosynthesis (Chapter 4). Psychosynthesis emphasises detachment from many different manifestations of the Self (our

[1] G. Sommerhoff 'The Abstract Characteristics of Living Systems' in F. E. Emery, *Systems Thinking*

[2] For a detailed discussion of the difference between the Systems notion of the steady state or dynamic homeostasis and equilibrium see Chapter 13

[3] F. E. Emery *Systems Thinking*, p. 10

sub-personalities) in order to know and realize the true Self. Now the individual who identifies with his various sub-personalities will be totally unable to maintain a simple direction and, therefore, equanimity, because each sub-personality will be directed towards a different end. It is only when the true Self appears to act as the conductor of the orchestra, that true unidirectionality is possible. It is interesting here to note that Jack Nicklaus's teacher, Jack Grant, had the following to say about his famous pupil: 'He was more single minded than any youngster I've ever known has been about anything – even the opposite sex.'[1] Nicklaus had isolated his true Self and was totally dedicated to reaching it. He had 'a conductor for his orchestra'.

Condition (b) was discussed in Chapter 5 where we argued that while we tend to operate normally at a level considerably lower than our true potential we must move steadily and without strain towards that potential. The earlier discussion related to the use of the body during the practice of yoga asanas. These two conditions can only be achieved by 'leadership and commitment'[2] or in other words 'conscious control'.

## *Golfing Goals and Systems Needs*

One of the biggest problems facing the individual is that there are so many people telling him in many different ways, some subtle, some less so, the goals that he should have and the direction he should take in his life. The family is probably the most powerful influence but society and friends also have their say. The result is often that the individual knows what *others* want but not what he himself wants.

Having goals that are not right for us leads to forcing and tension. Reaching the *wrong* goal needs a lot of will-power and gritting of teeth, whereas if we have the right goal we seem to move towards it with ease and enjoyment.

These notions can be further developed within the framework of some excellent work on this subject by Abraham Maslow, the humanistic psychologist. Maslow looks at the goal-oriented behaviour of the living system from the point of view of the *needs* of the human organism and has developed a theory of human motivation which postulates certain basic human needs. Maslow has isolated five in particular, these should be seen as hierarchical, in the sense

[1] J. Nicklaus *Golf My Way*, p. 9
[2] F. E. Emery *Systems Thinking*, p. 10

that as the lower, more basic, needs are satisfied, then, and only then, higher ones will emerge. Starting with the more basic needs we have:

1) Physiological Needs: feeding, sleeping, sex, etc.
2) Safety Needs: security, stability, freedom from fear and anxiety.
3) Belonging and Love Needs: friends, lovers, family, etc.
4) Esteem Needs: in Maslow's words 'all people in our society (with a few pathological exceptions) have a need or desire for a stable, firmly based, usually high, evaluation of themselves, for self-respect, or self-esteem, or for the esteem of others'.[1]
5) Needs for Self Actualization; the individual needs to develop and fulfil his partiular capacities and talents. 'A musician must make music, an artist must paint, a poet must write, if he is to be ultimately at peace with himself. What a man can be, he must be. He must be true to his own nature.'[1]

Thus the golfer is faced with a situation of harmonizing his needs with his goals. The failure to do just this creates the tension and lack of equilibrium. More particularly, the task is one of breaking away from those externally given goals and of satisfying more basic needs until a situation is reached where the true need harmonizes with the true goal: to realize the true Self.

*Basic Needs and Higher Needs and Golf*

The organism's needs can be satisfied either through the actual game of golf or through those institutions we have built around the game: principally, of course, the golf club. Our main golfing institution will be considered at a later state (Chapter 16) but it remains to investigate how far golf can and does satisfy some of our deeper needs. There is no doubt that some of the following points will offer insights into just why the game often has such a powerful hold on the individual.

The physiological and safety needs do not have much relevance in the golfing context except that the failure to satisfy them will distract the golfer and hold him back from satisfying his higher needs. There is no doubt that lack of security, say at home or at work, can have a disastrous effect on the golfer's performance. Likewise, hunger or the wish to go to the toilet will have an adverse effect from the physiological point of view.

The third level in Maslow's hierarchy – belonging and love – features strongly with the golfer who plays for social reasons. What seems important is that these social aspects should be recognized

[1] A. H. Maslow *Motivation and Personality*, pp. 45-6

and enjoyed to the full. There is a great tendency in our competitive world to become so obsessed with performance that the social side is overlooked.

The next need – esteem – figures in two powerful ways in the game of golf. One relates to the institutional side of the game – where being a member of a particular club confers social prestige and respect on the golfer. This was obvious at an exclusive County Club in Chicago where I worked one summer. The second way in which golf can confer a positive self-image on the golfer is through the appropriation of positive feedback from others after a successful performance on the course. In a culture that emphasizes success, this is possibly the most important, single, motivating factor.

The last of Maslow's needs hardly requires separate consideration. The goal of realizing your potential as a golfer is the basic theme of this book. All the techniques and methods suggested and discussed are felt, in their unique ways, to be means of helping the golfer towards this potential. What Maslow is saying, however, is that this 'highest' goal is intimately related to the highest need.

### *Deficiency Needs, Growth Needs and Golf*

Maslow's work on motivation and needs is worth considering further. He was able to distinguish between two important categories of motivation depending on the particular system need that predominated in the individual. His distinctions have interesting and significant implications for the golfing bodymind. Maslow found from his studies that he could distinguish between individuals motivated primarily by the needs for safety, love and self-esteem (deficiency or lower needs) and those motivated by the needs to develop their talents and capacities (growth or higher needs). He discovered that the motivations of people in the latter category were very different from those of the individual motivated primarily by the lower, more basic, needs. There was, in fact, a 'great gap' or divide. In discussing these differences it will become evident that several of the characteristics possessed by people interested primarily in growth are highly desirable in golf.

#### Gratification of Growth Needs:

Satisfying growth needs, according to Maslow, leads to increased motivation. In golf this means that the more you succeed in expressing your true potential as a golfer the more you will want to repeat the experience.

This explains Tony Jacklin's comment that one of the key factors in Jack Nicklaus's career was his 'fresh mental outlook' (see Chapter 6). Nicklaus is motivated primarily by fulfilling his talents as a golfer, and the experience of doing so increases rather than decreases his motivation. Hence the fresh mental outlook. Nicklaus is clearly a self-actualizer.

Dependence of the Environment:
The satisfaction of lower needs is only possible through other people, which means dependence on them and/or dependence on the environment. The growth-motivated individual, on the other hand, is not dependent and is, therefore, more autonomous and self-sufficient. The importance of the golfer being the 'independent variable' in his relationship with the environment has frequently been stressed because the system is considerably easier to control than the environment. Tony Jacklin was quoted recently as being favourably impressed by a few of the successful newcomers to the British tour who were loners, going their own way and not spending their time in groups or cliques. The point being that out on the course the golfer will certainly be on his own. Being growth-motivated encourages this independence.

Transcending the Ego:
Maslow has found that the growth-oriented person is best able to overcome his self-consciousness and concentrate on the problem in hand. This ability, of course, is at the heart of any zen approach to sport. It is basically the ability completely to trust our biological nature and to make the correct responses to environmental stimuli.

This leads to greater spontaneity and enables the creative, more natural, aspects of the individual to appear. Such increased spontaneity, argues Maslow, is evident in the growth-motivated individual. Murphy emphasizes its great importance on the golf course: 'All skill involves a certain measure of spontaneity and unconscious functioning; no-one can create beauty, be it in a work of art or on a golf links, unless he has both disciplined control and the ability to let go to the sudden glimmer.' And further: 'Inspiration and spontaneity must be given their place if any game is to be mastered and enjoyed.'[1]

Peak Experience:
Maslow has shown that peak experiences occur with greater frequency among self-actualizing individuals. Golfing peak moments have already been discussed in some detail (see Chapter 7)

[1] M. Murphy *Golf in the Kingdom*, pp. 194–5

when Tony Jacklin's 'cocoon of concentration' in which he became 'invincible' seemed the most accurate description of such an experience.

Nature of Perception:
The perception of growth-oriented individuals tends to be more clear, detached and penetrating. Since they have no reservations about their goals and aspirations, their thoughts are not filled with doubt and criticism. This state of mind is similar to the zen concept of non-judgemental awareness.

From Maslow's work it is clear that if the fulfilment of your potential in golf is the primary motivating factor, this is both desirable in itself and seems to lead to certain qualities which have value in themselves and in relation to golf.

What is also abundantly clear is that there is a world of difference between playing golf to boost your ego or self-image and playing golf as a means of expressing your talents and reaching your full potential both as a golfer and as a human being. When the game is played for purposes of self-actualization it seems to take on a purer form, becoming more like a true art.

## *Defining the Desire to Reach Our Golfing Goals*

The whole question of desire and motive is so important it is useful to categorize the different states of desire which are possible on the golf course because as golfers we will, at any one time, be at some particular point on the 'continuum of desire'. This will show the extent to which an experienced state differs from an ideal state.

Here is a tentative classification of desires starting with the more negative ones.

Negative Desire – Wants to Lose:
a) *The Golfing Masochist* this is a somewhat neurotic state of mind where the golfer wants to lose so that he can feel even more sorry for himself. For instance, I remember three putting five times in a round and actually wanting to three putt again. I wanted to increase my misery.
b) *The Golfing Altruist* In this case the golfer does not wish to succeed because he feels sorry for the opponent or because he feels kindly disposed towards him. The only criticism I can level against this attitude is that most opponents would rather beat someone who is

trying his hardest, rather than someone who is not. Not giving it all one has seems to devalue the game.

Neutral Desire – Apathy:
a) *The Social Golfer* This golfer plays for social reasons and the result of the game is largely incidental to the social encounter.
b) *The Health/Fun Oriented Golfer* Again success or the lack of it is incidental.
c) *The Super-Talent* Very talented golfers seem to become apathetic about their performance in competitions or appearances that are of little personal consequence to them. Usually a temporary state of affairs, however, and the golfer can easily change to a different level on the continuum.

Confused Desire – Don't Know:
a) *The Confused Golfer* There are aspects of success which may not appeal to the golfer – speeches, fame, social engagements and it seems quite possible that part of the golfer wants to win and another wants to lose.
b) *The Pressurized Golfer* Golfers are sometimes forced by parents or club members to go out and play. They themselves do not know whether they want to do so.
c) *The Drifter* This category includes the golfer who has drifted into the golfing arena without really thinking why or what for.
d) *The Golfer with Problems* Golfers with pressing business or family problems tend to be neutral about their golfing performance. Their desire to succeed on the golf course is dependent on the extent to which their problems are occupying their thoughts. This leads to an unsatisfactory sitution of opposing energies.

Wishful Desire – Hopes to Succeed:
a) *The Hopeful Golfer* The golfer in this very important category tends either to be hoping not to lose or hoping to win. Either way there are strong overtones of negativity in this state. In many cases it is to be preceded by the knowledge that failure is imminent. This state is certainly very different from positively wanting to win or succeed. Emery, in his book *Actualizations* puts it beautifully when he says 'Hope is the expectation that some source external to ourselves is going to save our ass so we will live happily ever after.'[1]

Positive Desire – Wants to Succeed:
a) *For Society* The Western world demands success. R. D. Laing has

[1] Stewart Emery *Actualizations* p. 37

referred to the process whereby these demands are 'internalized'.[1] The individual wants for himself what society wants of him. Even so, this state is less positive than those described below.
b) *For the Ego/Self-Image* The golfer in this category is motivated by his basic need for self-respect and the esteem of others. This is, however, desire of any order lower than that outlined in c) and d) below.
c) *For the Self* The desire to use and fulfil one's talents and capacities and to realize one's true potential is the primary motivating factor. This golfer is a 'self-actualizer' and moves towards satisfying this need through the medium of golf.
d) *For Others, e.g. Club, Country* Certain people are motivated more by success for a team than for themselves. The team may be a club or a national side but there is no doubt that for some golfers being on a team can be an expression of their potential. It can certainly be a very strong motivating factor. One example is when Brian Huggett burst into tears when he holed a five foot putt at Royal Birkdale, which he thought would win Britain the Ryder Cup.

Within these four categories it is possible to use certain adjectives to describe the strength of the desire to be successful as weak, strong, very strong and, even, too strong.

The real significance of this discussion is the close relationship between desire and effort. Desire to succeed affects closely the effort expended on the golf course and is a crucial factor in determining performance. Indeed, the whole Western approach to sport stresses the importance of effort and highly commends hard work and will-power. There is much in this. The point, however, is that it tends to be taken to excess and a stage is reached where more effort leads to fewer results. This is where the progress by less method comes into effect. But suddenly changing how hard you try is no easy matter and would seem to be something that can only be done gradually. A quantum leap from one level of desire to another is just not possible. However, all the methods and approaches I have discussed are ways, either directly or indirectly, of affecting desire and motivation. And, indeed, simply being aware of where you lie on the continuum is likely to provide a positive impetus.

## *Reaching Those Golfing Goals*

It will be obvious that it is one thing to have goals and quite another

1. R. D. Laing *The Politics of the Family*

to reach them. And what is not always fully appreciated by those selecting and choosing their goals is the total committment needed to actually realize any meaningful goal. Indeed, if the full implications were realized at the start, there is little doubt that many would never begin!

What is also in little doubt, however, is that very many will fail on the way. In spite of this, it is worthwhile recalling some words spoken by Tony Jacklin as he set off for his first venture on the American golf circuit. He said something to the effect that even if he failed, he would be able to live with himself in the knowledge that he gave it a bloody good go. What mattered was participating.

Though participating is indeed ultimately what is important many fail because they do not fully appreciate the various stages that are involved in the actual realization of a serious and important goal. These stages are excellently outlined by Robert Assagioli. [1]

Assagioli isolates the six sequential phases involved in an act of will: [2]

1) The Purpose, Aim, or Goal based on Evaluation, Motivation, and Intention.
2) Deliberation.
3) Choice and Decision.
4) Affirmation; the Command, or 'Fiat' of the Will.
5) Planning and Working Out a Programme.
6) Direction of the Execution. [3]

Let us assume for the present that the first three stages have been covered and the goal selected is 'to reach full potential in the game of golf.' This purpose will have been chosen from a number of options.

The next stage in the Act of Will is *Affirmation.* This stage is important as it adds weight and power to the decision. It is basically a case of reaffirming your choice. Assagioli suggests certain techniques which can be used:

a) The use of 'words of power'. Actually use the name of a feared opponent or say to yourself the team you wish to get on – Walker Cup, Ryder Cup, etc., and keep saying them to yourself. These words can be really evocative. Try and see!

[1] Robert Assagioli *The Act of Will*, p. 135

[2] If we accept Wilber's definition of the *Will* as a 'three dimensional act of the total organism to globally move in time towards some future end', it becomes clear that the realization of one's golfing potential is certainly an act of will.

[3] Robert Assagioli *The Act of Will*, p. 135

b) The use of images. Visualize yourself as the successful golfer you wish to become. Imagine yourself 'as if' you had succeeded, or use De Ropp's 'mental theatre'. This technique has already been discussed. (See Chapter 4.)
c) Assume physical attitudes. Walk and behave like the top golfers, i.e. act 'as if'.

Next is the *planning* stage. As Assagioli points out, many of us find ourselves planning and programming at our jobs but remain reluctant to carry out the same procedures with our own lives. Nevertheless 'careful planning and patient execution of a life plan and subplans are necessary if one is to fulfil (one's) personal existence and become all that (one) can'. [1]

The golfer who seemed to pay most attention to this matter was Ben Hogan. According to Gene O'Brien, who studied Hogan over 25 years, 'he was the master of planning and preparation. In his approach to the game he was, first and foremost, an architect. By that I mean he designed his swing and game to play each course, in turn, as his prime opponent.' [2] In golf it is not only one's game that has to be organized but the various non-golfing activities that surround it. If plans are not made to handle these they can act as distractions; for example, business and social commitments, as well as getting oneself, plus caddie, plus equipment at the right time to the right place, in the right state of mind. Poor preparation can destroy much of the good work done in the other aspects involved.

The final stage is the *direction of the execution*. In Assagioli's words:

> ... the true and natural function of the will at this stage is to direct the execution, to put into operation the necessary and appropriate means for reaching the proposed objective. It does so by taking command of and directing the various psychophysical functions'. [3]

This is the stage where the golfer is out on the course on his own. It is quite possibly the last nine holes of a big event. Here lie the greatest opportunities for giving expression of our true potential. Success actually depends, as Assagioli points out, on the co-ordination of the mind and the body, the emotions and feelings. This needs a will both strong and skilful. While it should be recognized that in this last stage the golfer will be left to his own devices, Assagioli has devised certain techniques, some of which

[1] R. Assagioli *The Act of Will*, p. 185
[2] Gene O'Brien *Golf Monthly*, Junne1977
[3] R. Assagioli *The Act of Will*, p. 189

have been covered, which help in the development of the skill and strength of the will.

SUMMARY

This chapter has considered in some detail one of the most important 'common characteristics' of the living system. To consider the characteristics that are common to all open systems is a distinguishing feature of a Systems approach to a problem. In this case the characteristic of goal orientation in golf has been studied.

We also looked at several important dimensions of goal-oriented behaviour, stressing in particular the importance of having goals which satisfy the needs of the golfing bodymind. These needs have been outlined by Abraham Maslow and the conclusion reached was that the highest golfing goal, that of fulfilling your golfing potential, corresponds to the highest of the Systems needs: the need for self-actualization.

In the discussion of goals, the question of 'systems needs' is vital because as a need emerges so does the desire to satisfy that need. The significance of desire is highlighted when the great Jack Nicklaus chooses desire as the most important of all the factors responsible for success on the golf course. He concludes in *Golf My Way* that 'if you have enough of that (desire) it's amazing what you can do at golf, or in any other area of life for that matter.' [1]

While the argument of this book focuses more on the individual reaching his potential than any actual victory or external achievement through golf, the position of desire and motivation remains central.

If Nicklaus has isolated the secret of success he has highlighted a problem for us: to know our real desires is not easy. Maslow makes this quite clear: '... to know what one really is, and what one *really* wants is a rare and high culmination that comes infrequently and that usually takes long years of courage and hard work.'

It is in recognition of what is involved that Assagioli outlines the six stages involved in an act of will. It remains for the golfer to see the stages through. To actually do so is to realize our highest goal.

[1] J. Nicklaus *Golf My Way*, p. 255

## RECOMMENDED FURTHER READING

1) R. Assagioli *The Act of Will*
2) R. Assagioli *Psychosynthesis*
3) A. H. Maslow *Motivation and Personality*
4) A. H. Maslow *Towards a Psychology of Being*
5) David Campbell *If You Don't Know Where You're Going, You'll Probably End Up Somewhere Else*

# *Chapter Ten*

## SYSTEMS QUALITY I – CONCENTRATION

*'He thought of one thing at a time – the shot in hand.'*

Of Vardon *'His concentration always struck me as wonderful. He seemed to sink into the game.'*

Concentration is one of the Systems qualities that were isolated in attempting to answer a question of the Systems approach. The question asked which qualities enabled 'the system' to survive in its defined environment. What this meant in practice was a consideration of those factors which enabled the system to survive various crises in its environment, in our case, defined as that of the tournament golfer. The basic argument being that surviving the pressure in golf has far more to do with the internal world of the golfers than with technique. Under pressure even the best techniques can falter, the finest swings fall apart. We shall now discuss the qualities necessary for the golfer if he is to overcome these moments of internal weakness.

### *Concentration and Goals*

Concentration means the focussing of attention, which presupposes the presence of something on which to focus, in this case the relevant golfing goals. It is well known that telling yourself to concentrate simply does not work. What is often not appreciated though is that the root cause of the failure to concentrate is either the lack of a goal on which to concentrate or the inability of the chosen goal to absorb or satisfy the golfing bodymind. The problem of goals given to the individual by family or society has already been strongly emphasized. Once that 'true' goal is found, concentration, it seems, ceases to be a problem.

To support this we can refer to Maslow again. The self-actualizer, he found, has the ability to concentrate to a degree not usual for ordinary men.[1] He is able, as we have said, to concentrate on the problem, with which he is faced. Self-actualisers are 'problem centred' rather than 'ego centred'.

Maslow was also able to describe just what it means to really concentrate: 'This may be called "total attention" ... What I am trying to describe here is very much akin to fascination or complete absorption.'

Andra Kirkaldy also has an excellent description when he says of Harry Vardon: 'he seemd to sink into the game'. In yoga, there is actually a term, *dhyana,* to describe this state when the object of concentraton completely fills the mind, when the game and the player are one. Georg Fuerstein puts it like this:

> All arising ideas gyrate round the object of concentration and are accomplished by an emotive disposition which can be described as "peaceful" or "calm". There is no loss of lucidity, rather the sense of wakefulness appears to be intensified.[2]

This description has several striking similarities with Jacklin's peak golfing moments previously discussed. To repeat:

> It's not like playing golf in a dream or anything like that. Quite the opposite. When I'm in this state everything is pure, vividly clear.

These descriptions are useful for they provide a means of assessing the extent to which we differ from the ideal. If we find ourselves unable to concentrate on the golf course it could be a time for some deep thinking about our goals and directions. Maybe our bodymind is trying to tell us something – perhaps we have lost our sense of perspective. We have certainly lost our enthusiasm for the game and perhaps need a break. Indeed one of the golfing wise men who spent an evening with Michael Murphy philosophizing about the game goes so far as to suggest we should give up the game. 'There's no use playin',' he says, 'if the fascination doesna' take ye.'[3]

### *Concentration – the Phenomenon of the Headless Golfer*

Few golfers would dispute the importance of concentration and

[1] A. H. Maslow *Motivation and Personality*, p. 161
[2] G. Fuerstein *Textbook of Yoga*, p. 130
[3] M. Murphy *Golf in the Kingdom*, p. 62

some even go so far as to suggest it is the most common of golfing problems. What is basically happening is that one is on the course in a physical sense but mentally elsewhere; hence, *the phenomenom of the headless golfer.* It is as if the mind and body are leading two separate existences, similar to when you arrive home and do not remember any of the previous fifteen minutes or so because your mind was elsewhere.

There are two basic types of headlessness amongst golfers:

a) Horizontal
This category relates to the common malaise of spending time regretting that missed shot or missed putt on the previous hole: this may be called *backward headlessness.* Closely related to this is the time spent thinking of the birdies or disasters of the forthcoming holes. It also includes time spent planning the acceptance speech at the presentation: this is *forward headlessness.*

b) Vertical
Vertical headlessness relates to mind-wandering due to the various 'other' aspects of our life that are allowed to intrude during the game, and particularly when they are causing worry or concern.

Arnold Palmer was one of the great golfers who knew this well; he used to make sure things were happy with his wife Winnie and his family before a tournament. He understood how potentially distracting these off-the-course matters can be. Palmer, it will be recalled (Chapter 1), felt that the thing he did best on the golf course was to concentrate, so he may be regarded as something of an expert on this matter. The widespread recognition of this point amongst the golfing community might mean an end to the plight of the long-suffering 'golfer's widow'. The lonely spouse would do well to recommend the Systems approach to her 'better half' for the argument here is that a happy home will tend to mean a happy golfer. The interplay between life at home and life on the course just will not be severed.

### *How to Develop Concentration*

While there is no doubt that the golfer's ability to concentrate on his game is related primarily to the strength of his motivation to reach his golfing goals, there are some practical steps that can be taken to improve and develop the ability to concentrate. These techniques are perhaps more a question of making the golfer *aware* of the fact that he is not concentrating than of actually improving his inherent capacity to attend to the job on hand. Learning to become aware that your thoughts are wandering is clearly the first step towards improving concentration.

The actual methods chosen can be split into those that can be practised off the course and those that can be practised on the course:

Off the Course

Practising concentration is very easy in one sense and very difficult in another. It is easy because all you have to do is select some object or thing – a candle, a cup or even a golf ball – sit comfortably and just start concentrating. (Billie Jean King apparently used to practice looking at a tennis ball.) It is difficult because you will probably soon realize that you just cannot do it. You will realize in fact that you have very little control over your thoughts and that you are only able to concentrate for a matter of seconds before your mind wanders off. These 'eel-like' qualities of the mind have already been described in the chapter on yoga (Chapter 5) where concentration was put forward as an important method of trapping the 'eel'. Another excellent object of concentration is the breath. It forms, in fact, the basis of zazen meditation exercises in Zen Buddhism. In zazen meditation the participant is told to sit erect in a cross-legged position and to simply count the number of breaths. The breath, as we have said before, is seen in Eastern culture as being the key to the control of mind and body. It is mastery of the breath that unites the mind and body, moving the individual to Level III, the Existential level developed earlier (Chapter 6). Zazen meditation certainly increases the awareness of the breath and this awareness as we have suggested can be a means of controlling anxiety and tension during the round.

The other important 'off the course' method of improving concentration is to improve your health. All the books on the subject agree on this matter. Alexander saw mind-wandering on the golf course as the result of the mis-use of the psycho-physical organism. Improving the use of the bodymind, would, he argued, improve concentration.

Maslow also stressed this point though he put more emphasis on the psychological aspects of health. Maslow saw his basic needs (physiological, safety, love and belongingness and an acceptable self-image) as being as essential to the bodymind as salt or water. For him psychological health is dependent on the extent to which these needs are satisfied. We have also explained earlier how the golfer's motivation toward reaching his potential is dependent on the satisfaction of these needs and how closely related were motivational factors and ability to concentrate.

## On the Course

There is, of course, no reason why practice sessions or the very playing of the game cannot be used as an opportunity to develop powers of concentration. Ben Hogan was probably the golfer who made best use of this opportunity. As Gene O'Brien recalls:

> Hogan, through the process of learning, found that you cannot turn your concentration on and off at will ... he played each shot as if it were the most important shot he had ever hit, and his attitude was the same when he hit his 250 shots in a session on the practice tee, or with the shots he played in a practice round. He trained himself to play at his "best" pressure at all times, even in practice.[1]

Timothy Gallwey, writing with respect to tennis, suggests we must develop our love for the object of concentration, making the game a form of Bhakti yoga, which is the yoga of love and devotion. He also suggests focusing attention on something subtle within the game such as the spin of the ball or the sound the ball makes when it hits the racket. These are techniques which can certainly be applied to golf.

## SUMMARY

For Gallwey 'concentration' is the supreme art because no art can be achieved without it, while with it, anything can be achieved.[2] This sentence, while being beautifully simple, perhaps makes us forget temporarily just what is involved in the total concentration of the bodymind on our chosen goal. It is, as we have seen, a question, primarily, of motivation, which in turn depends on the extent to which we have satisfied lower, basic System needs isolated by Maslow. A brief consideration was given to practical techniques which can be applied both on and off the golf course to develop this 'supreme art'.

## RECOMMENDED FURTHER READING

1) A. H. Maslow *Motivation and Personality*
2) Ernest Wood *Concentration*
3) Mouni Sadhu *Concentration*

[1] *Golf Monthly* June 1977
[2] T. Gallwey *The Inner Game of Tennis*

# *Chapter Eleven*

# SYSTEMS QUALITY II – EQUANIMITY

*'What golf-writers call "temperament" – a thing we hear far too much about – I just call common sense.'*
*'The great thing was to enjoy the game and not to go round the links in a bad temper because you could not beat "bogey".'*

## *Equanimity and Attachment*

That the Systems quality of equanimity is at the opposite end of a continuum from anxiety, our golfing enemy number one, has already been discussed at some length (Chapter 3). The key to affecting a move in either direction along this continuum lies in the concept of *attachment*. It is such an important concept that it is here discussed again but from the particular viewpoint of the golfer – including it as part of the Systems theoretical framework.

### Attachment and the Ego-Mind

During the first part of the argument an apparent inconsistency emerged. Half the techniques introduced seemed to be arguing for positive egos and positive self-images while the other half were arguing that the thought processes of the ego-mind merely hinder the human organism from realizing its full potential. A reconciliation was attempted by postulating different levels of awareness and suggesting that while a technique may be very relevant at one level it may well have little or no application at another (Chapter 6).

Thus, for a golfer at Level I which has been called the 'No Game Level', creating an integrated, positive and healthy ego will constitute the major task. Though this will eventually have to be abandoned at the third and fourth level, it constitutes a vital step in the golfer's inner evolution. This is because the inner progress must be made slowly ('within limits defined as reasonable') and it is

'He was more single minded than any youngster I've ever known has been about anything – even the opposite sex.'

*Jack Grant, Jack Nichlaus's teacher*

'One of the key factors in his career . . . much more than he is given credit for is his mental outlook, his fresh mental outlook.'

— *Tony Jacklin on Jack Nicklaus*

'. . . the pure fact that you go out on the first tee of a tournament and say, "I must concentrate today" is no good. It won't work. It must be there already.'

— *Tony Jacklin*

'Everything came into focus. Although I could feel my club at every half-inch of my swing, I was free from thinking about various parts of my game.'

– *Tony Jacklin*

' . . . We are presently using only ten per cent of our brain's capabilities in golf.'
*– Johnny Miller*

'I just cannot be satisfied with anything less than the best in condition and performance of which I know I am capable.'

– *Gary Player*

Lee Trevino, gripped by tension at his winning putt, goes into a frenzy of excitement.

BOBBY LOCKE

'Bobby Locke was a golfer with an amazingly even temperament. He did everything quietly and in slow motion.'

– *Gary Player*

When asked what he did best Arnold Palmer replied, 'Concentrate'.

Gary Player described himself as 'the fittest 35-year-old in the world'.

necessary to build a stable and healthy base from which to move towards the higher and more demanding levels. Steps in the evolution through the levels cannot simply be omitted without risk.

It must also be appreciated that while the ego-mind itself is a cause of anxiety, the development of the integrated, positive ego represents a considerable improvement on the mind that identifies solely with whatever sub-personality, good or bad, happens to be in the driving seat at any particular moment. The healthy ego indicates the developing ability to differentiate and control the various aspects of the self to a particular end. This increased control inevitably means less distress and confusion and, therefore, less anxiety.

### Attachment and other Emotions

The game of golf gives rise to a whole range of emotions. Anxiety is the most important but it is only one of many. Anger, excitement, joy, despair and frustration all play their part. They all have to be integrated for the golfer to have control over them. The key to doing so lies not in suppressing these powerful emotions but in recognizing their existence through the practice of detachment. Simply accepting the negative emotion, whatever it may be, seems to make it lose its power.

### Attachment and your Goals

The importance of goals has been repeatedly stressed in this book. They have been seen as a crucial motivating factor and essential prerequisite to the golfer's ability to realize his potential. Goals are the first step in the exercise of *will* (Chapters 4 and 9). And an act of will, it will be recalled, is a positive decision and an expression of control.

What must be realized is that the golfer must even remain detached from his chosen goals. This notion is best explained by reference to Alexander's work on the dangers of 'end-gaining'. For him, the principal problem was that our 'end-gaining' acts meant that we often overlooked the best means by which we could achieve our goal.

## *Equanimity and the Body*

The importance of the body in controlling emotional states has been noted. Robert S. De Ropp in *The Master Game* argues that 'the key to the control of the emotional centre lies in the moving centre'. Walter Carrington in an article entitled 'Balance as a Function of Intelligence' shows that 'Physical balance and psychological balance are bound up closely together. Equipoise and equanimity go hand in hand.'

These insights are very useful for there is no doubt that it is very difficult to control any given emotional state. Because of the physical manifestations of the emotions, however, action can be taken. The control of the particular state of muscular tension is especially useful to the golfer, for this will have a corresponding effect on the emotion. The relative state of tension of a muscle can be split into three categories:

*Hypo-tonic State* – completely relaxed
*Tonic State* – a state of readiness
*Hyper-tonic State* – a state of excess tension

These 'relative states' should be taught by any good teacher of Hatha yoga. This will make the golfer aware of tension in his muscles and also put him in a position he learns to control. Clearly, on the golf course, the hyper-tonic state can have a disastrous effect on his swing. Ideally the golfer should be in the hypo-tonic state between shots, changing to the tonic state for the shot. The other aspect of Hatha yoga that is of relevance to anxiety on the golf course is breathing. (See Chapter 5.)

*Equanimity and the Mind*

One well-known method of countering an emotional state, particularly anger, is counting to ten. This has the advantage, like breathing, of taking the golfer's attention from what he has just done to something more mundane. It brings him from the past into the present.

Another technique which can certainly work is autosuggestion: simply telling yourself that you are relaxed. Practice lying on the floor at home and telling each part of your body to relax in turn. Say to yourself 'my feet are heavy' – feel them getting heavy; 'my feet are relaxing' – feel yourself relaxing. Obviously it is not so easy to lie down on the course but the same approach can be used even when standing up.

Dr David Morley suggests a technique which uses the mind's powers of imagination. Imagining the body as a receptacle containing a psychic fluid which represents the anxiety. The exercise is to imagine the fluid slowly flowing out of the receptacle.

Yet another method is the skilled use of the various subpersonalities we all have and discovered by psychosynthesis. If 'Mr

Anxious' sub-personality is the forefront you can call on others such as Mr Brave or Mr Courageous, and you might find Mr Anxious beating a rapid retreat. It might help to associate your positive sub-personalities with symbols or images related to the nature of the personalities. Mr Brave, for example, might be lion-like. Warriors of the ancient world are reported to have used such imagery and wore lion and tiger skins as well as horns and fangs to associate themselves with strength. It is a question of using your imagination.

*Equanimity and Self-Discipline*

If we widen the perspective to the golfer's entire life, we see that the individual's ability to handle himself when the going gets rough is also due to self discipline. Being strict with yourself at the right time seems to develop the inner strength which helps maintain control when the environment gets hard on you. Recognizing the importance of self discipline, the psychologist William James suggests the technique of performing useless exercises. In an excellent passage from his book *Talks to Teachers*, he offers the following advice:

> Keep the facility of effort alive in you by a little gratuituous exercise everyday. That is, be systematically heroic in little unnecessary points; do every day or two something for no other reason than its difficulty, so that, when the hour of dire need draws nigh, it may find you not unnerved to stand the test. Asceticism of this sort is like the insurance which a man pays on his house and goods. The tax does him no good at the time, and possibly may never bring him a return. But, if fire does come, his having paid it, it will be his salvation from ruin. So with the man who has daily inured himself to habits of concentrated attention, energetic volition, and self-denial in unnecessary things. He will stand like a tower when everything rocks around him, and his softer fellow mortals are rocked in the blast.[1]

*Equanimity and Success – 'the Jonah Complex'*

Many golfers will be surprised to hear that what disturbs equanimity on the golf course is not fear of failing as is commonly supposed, but fear of success. The famous humanistic psychologist Abraham Maslow calls this the Jonah Complex and writes:

> We fear our highest possibilities (as well as our lowest ones).

[1] Quoted in R. Assagioli *Psychosynthesis*, p. 133

> We are generally afraid to become that which we can glimpse in our most perfect moments, under the most perfect conditions, under conditions of greatest courage. We enjoy and even thrill to the god-like possibilities we see in ourselves in such peak moments. And yet we simultaneously shiver with weakness, awe and fear before these same possibilities.[1]

The recognition of this fear of the sublime adds weight to the importance of visual rehearsal of successful performance. At present few golfers practice visualization systematically although many who achieve success use the technique instinctively at times. The reason Jack Nicklaus was walking down the 18th at St Andrews as the 1978 British Champion is that he had been there before – mentally. He had by rehearsal overcome the fear of success that seemed to strike the man who had been in the lead at the 16th; the little known New Zealnder Simon Owen.

### *Equanimity and the Self*

We may feel we are in control of our emotions and able to 'keep our heads'. The real test, however, as William James so rightly points out, is when 'everything rocks around' or, in the golfer's case, when faced with the 'crisis situation' – a situation that is inevitable as we move towards our edge.

What is absolutely certain is that golf has a remarkable ability to knock the individual from that state of 'control'. This is inevitable and nobody, no matter how calm they may appear, is immune.

The important point, however, is to be able to bounce back, to return to the fight and not to give up. This ability is only really possible if the golfer has a centre, some point of reference to cling to in the wild environment in which he will find himself as he moves towards his peak. That centre is, of course, the true Self – the inner vision that can guide us through the rough and the smooth (see Chapter 4).

### SUMMARY

Our second Systems quality has been considered in this chapter from a theoretical and practical level. On the practical side a number of techniques were suggested, while on the theoretical side, equanimity has emerged intimately related to the emotion of anxiety, being at opposing ends of a continuum. The means of

[1] Maslow A. H. 'Neurosis as a Failure of Personal Growth' *Humanitas III*, 1966, pp. 153-69.

moving along this was shown to be detachment. Both theory and practice seem to get back to one thing, *awareness*, the subject of the next chapter.

## RECOMMENDED FURTHER READING

1) Rama, Ballentine and Ajaya *Yoga and Psychotherapy*
2) David C. Morley *The Missing Links – Golf and the Mind*
3) R. Assagioli *Psychosynthesis*
4) Bruno Geba *Breathe Away Your Tension; An Introduction to Gestalt Body Awareness Therapy*

# *Chapter Twelve*

## SYSTEMS QUALITY III – AWARENESS

*'To be a great golfer is all very well, but to play the game for the love of it and the good you get out of it – that is the main thing.'*

When the concept of awareness was chosen as one of the Systems qualities in the Introduction, its selection was justified because it was clearly of paramount importance to be *aware* in a physical sense of where you were in relation to the hole (external) as well as being aware of crucial feedback from the body (internal) which would provide the information about balance, timing or mis-timing the ball. As the argument of the book has developed, however, it has become apparent that awareness is a matter of significance beyond these purely physical aspects.

In fact, virtually every topic selected for discussion in this book revolves around the concept of self-awareness. The golfer's motivation, or will-to-succeed, is directly related to the extent to which that golfer is aware of, and able to satisfy, his basic needs. The discussions about concentration and equaniminity – our other two Systems qualities – have both led to the subject of awareness. The concept is clearly important in the physical, mental and emotional sense.

### *Thinking and Awareness*

The brain, in simple terms, is capable of two basic processes: it can think and it can be aware. It will have become very apparent that 'awareness' is needed on the golf course far more than 'thinking'. Professor Robert Ornstein has done some work on brain waves in California. Ornstein discovered that when he gave people particular tasks one side of the brain became active and the other passive. The activities associated with the left hand side (LHS) were language, logic, analytical thought – all, incidentally, the subjects emphasized by Western education. Right hand side (RHS) activities were rhythm, day-dreaming, images and imagination, feeling and intuition. Golf, of course is concerned largely with RHS activities. The importance of rhythm and the use of the images and imagination by means of the technique of creative visualization of shots has been stressed by many of the great golfers and teachers (see Chapter 4). We are, therefore, playing a game that is basically a RHS game, but we are exposed to a culture that values and stresses the development of the LHS of the brain.

The following table sets side-by-side these two processes of the brain and outlining their distinctive features – particularly those methods and techniques normally associated with the training of a particular mode. It will become quite apparent just how much the emphasis of this whole argument has been on the awareness mode; it is these RHS disciplines that the Western golfing world needs. It is here and only here, that we can begin to offset some of the imbalances that have characterized our approach to golf.

Significantly, Ornstein's work also revealed that if a LHS dominant person participated in RHS activities, and, therefore, developed the RHS, there was an improvement in the functioning of both sides of the brain. The LHS, in other words, operated more effectively as a result of participating in RHS activities. If the two sides were added together the whole was greater than the sum of its parts. This is *synergy* in operation again.

We can now discuss the popular observation that in order to play top quality golf it is necessary to be either very intelligent or very unintelligent.[1] This belief comes from recognizing that thinking processes are of little use on the golf course and that, presumably, it takes someone of high intelligence to realize this and, what's more, to abandon the thoughts that are holding him back from his potential. Presumably the LHS in very intelligent golfers is better controlled so that it does not act as a constraint or inhibitor.

Although it would seem that not using the LHS because of low intelligence may give advantages on the course, intelligence is still extremely important, not only because of the need for balance and the power of synergy, but because a certain intelligence is demanded to handle successfully the numerous 'off course' distractions. Peter Thompson once observed that it is the golfers who solve the problem

[1] Intelligence is taken here to be a term to describe an individual's relative proficiency at LHS activities

*The Functions and Characteristics of the Two sides of the Brain*

| | LHS | RHS |
|---|---|---|
| PRIMARY FUNCTION | THOUGHT | AWARENESS |
| PRINCIPAL ACTIVITIES | Analysis, language, logic. | Rhythm day-dreaming images/imagination feelings/intuition. |
| MODE OF OPERATION | Partial, dualistic, outward looking active/male /yang. | Holistic, systems, inward looking receptive/female/yin. |
| METHOD OF CLASSIFICATION WITHIN MODE | LEVEL OF INTELLIGENCE I.Q. test, examination qualifications. | LEVEL OF AWARENESS It is possible to isolate 4 distinct levels: *No Game level.* *Ego level* Awareness of mind. *Existential level* Awareness of mind and body. *Zen level* Awareness of mind, body and universe (see Chap. 6). |
| TECHNIQUES FOR DEVELOPMENT OF MODE | Training in the concepts and symbols of the scientific world. In golf, read books or articles on technique; go to the golf professional. | The appropriate technique depends on the level of awareness. *Ego level* Positive thinking, psychocybernetics, psychosynthesis, self-discipline (in yoga – yama and niyama).[1] *Existential level* Hatha yoga, Alexander Technique, meditation, concentration, breathing techniques. *Zen level* Zen Buddhism, Raja, Karma yoga – meditation. *At all levels* – viz. golf visualization, psychosynthesis. |

[1] Patanjali outlines the eight stages in the yogic path which makes it clear yama (restraint) and the niyama (self-discipline) must precede stages 3 and 4 – posture and breath control. See G. Fuerstein, *Textbook of Yoga* p. 124–34.

of how to fill the ten hours in the day that they are not playing golf who are the consistent winners.[1]

For the tournament golfer this refers particularly to the social, media and business pressures which have to be managed so that they do not distract from the primary purpose. Intelligence is also necessary in acquiring a sound knowledge of the technical side of the game. This knowledge must be sufficient to enable the golfer to act as his own doctor, his own mechanic. The basic regulation of the open system is self-regulation.

The conclusion, then, is clear. What is needed is a balance, for without it, we are something less than whole, something less than we can be. The evidence seems to bear this out for the world's truly great golfers appear to have effected this balance. They are said to be capable of doing anything well and from observation appear to be articulate, capable and interesting as well as being very talented and successful on the golf course. They are as RHS capable as they are LHS capable.

### *Awareness – The Different Perspectives*

#### Awareness and the Body

The importance of body awareness was discussed when exercises for golf were considered (Chapter 3). The main point being that in the choice of an exercise system consideration should be given to all the factors vital to golfing performance. Golfers tend to pay more attention to the strengthening of muscles in order to hit the ball a long way. This could sometimes merely increase the tension in the muscles which would reduce the feeling and sensations so important for rhythm and balance. Exercise systems which combine all aspects, such as Hatha yoga, have been suggested as the most appropriate. This discipline, in particular, was recommended because it combined the mental side in the performance of the exercise, recognizing the basic psychosomatic unity.

#### Awareness and Concentration

*Awareness* of the fact that you are not concentrating is the first step along the path to improving concentration. From another point of view, developing awareness is not possible without concentration. We have, then, two vital Systems qualities whose development can proceed hand-in-hand. Robert De Ropp puts it like this: 'Attention is to awareness, as the oil in a lamp is to its flame. While there is oil

[1] P. Thompson and D. Zwar *This Wonderful World of Golf*, p. 9

in the lamp, the flame persists, once the oil is exhausted the flame goes out.'[1]

Concentration and awareness have what is basically a 'chicken and egg' relationship. Developing one automatically develops the other. Awareness of a true inner goal provides intense inner

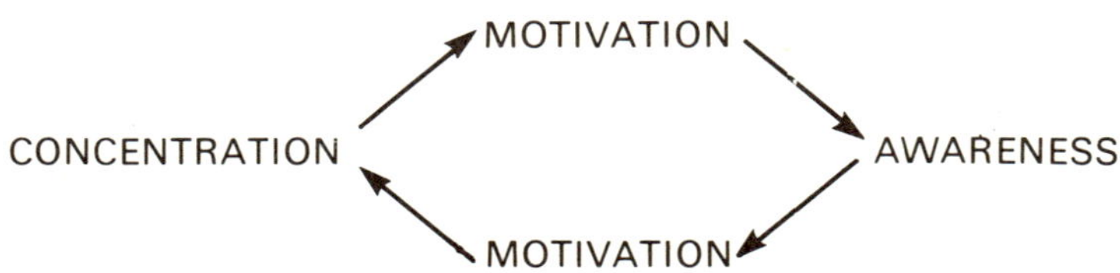


*Figure 1*

motivation and naturally focuses concentration (Chapter 9), which has long been recommended as a path to inner awareness and indeed occupies a central place in the yogic tradition (Chapter 5). One excellent example of this in top sport is four times Wimbledon champion Bjorn Borg, whose superb concentration is closely related to his strong inner drive.

Awareness and Equanimity

Equanimity is an emotional state. While it is extremely difficult to control a particular emotion (see Chapter 2) every emotion has physical manifestations which are more tangible and could provide the means to controlling the original emotion. The key to it all, however, is awareness of both the emotion and the means of control. Awareness in itself is a means of control. To quote De Ropp again:

> . . . the fact is . . . that observation, which means bringing a sensation into the focus of awareness, alters the process itself. It brings about a definite change in the nervous pathways that are operating to produce the anxiety. It switches the energy into a different channel.

So one who sets out with the intention: 'I am going to observe carefully the *physical sensations* of this thing I call "anxiety" ', discovers to his surprise that there is *no anxiety* left to observe.

Note that the anxiety is simply *observed*, not tackled directly. [2]

[1] Robert S. De Ropp *The Master Game*, p. 75
[2] R. S. De Ropp *The Master Game*

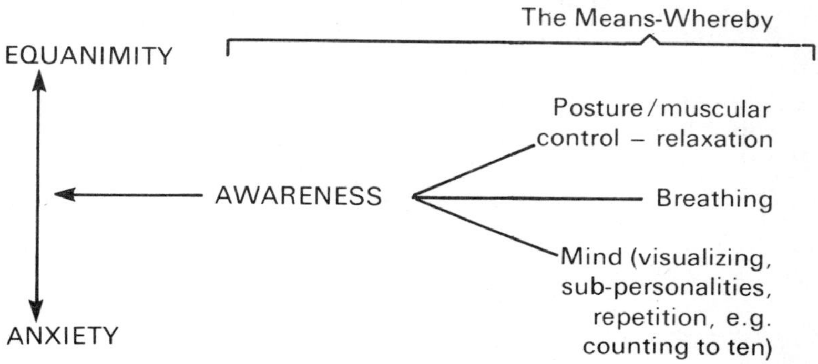


*Figure 2*

*Awareness as the Goal.*
The interrelationship between awareness and motivation has been discussed in connection with golfing goals. (See Chapter 9.) There is a school of thought which suggests that the pursuit of awareness should be seen as a golfing goal. This is implied in Alexander's strong and convincing arguments for the 'means-whereby' principle. It is also at the heart of Michael Murphy's *Golf in the Kingdom* and, indeed, the Eastern approach to sport. The basis of this approach is that achievement will be a natural and inevitable by-product of the pursuit of awareness, which is strongly supported by Maslow's hierarchical needs (Chapter 10).

*Altered States of Awareness*

Assuming the motivational emphasis of certain golfers does switch from achievement to awareness, it would seem relevant to give some indication of just where this new path might lead. To a certain extent this has been done already when an attempt was made to describe just what it meant to get all the parts working as one – Colin Wilson's state of 'full moon' (Chapter 7). The notion of altered states of awareness was put forward as a distinct possibility on the course. Indeed, their occurrence in certain other major sports was described in some detail. I shall now outline in a more definitive way characteristics of these altered states. Certain of Maslow's work will be used, for as he tells us: 'The great creators have described their creative moments in almost identical terms, even though they were various poets, chemists, sculptors, philosophers and mathematicians.'[1] Maslow, as has been pointed out already, concentrated his research on those individuals who had realized their particular potential.

## *Particular Characteristics of Altered States*

### Richer Perception

Perception during the peak experiences is very much richer and clearer than that normally experienced. Jacklin, for instance, said he felt his club at every half inch of his swing during his 'peak' at the end of the Lancôme Trophy. C. Leonard quotes John Brodie, the quarter-back in the San Francisco 49-ers, in his book, *The Ultimate Athlete*: 'Often, in the heat and excitement of a game, a player's perception and coordination will improve dramatically.'

### Loss of Fear

Kenneth Ravizza interviewed 20 athletes concerning their peak experiences in sport as a part of his doctoral programme at the University of Southern California and found that loss of fear was a quality felt by every one of his subjects. Maslow also noted 'a complete, though momentary, loss of fear, anxiety, inhibition, defense . . .'. [2]

### Emptiness

Michael Murphy describes a 'stupendous silence' that came upon him during a game of golf 'in which the other players, the golf course, the distant hills seemed suspended in air'.[3] This would tie in with Ian Thompson's experience as he entered the tunnel to win the marathon at the Commonwealth games (Chapter 7).

### Disorientation in Time and Space

Jacklin's peak experience involved a very definite disorientation of

[1] A. H. Maslow *Toward a Psychology of Being*, p. 85

[2] A. H. Maslow *Toward a Psychology of Being*, p. 94

[3] M. Murphy 'Sport as Yoga' *Journal of Humanistic Psychology*, Vol. 17, No. 4, 1977

time and space (see description, Chapter 7). This, too, has been described by John Brodie:

> time seem to slow down in an uncanny way, as if every one were moving in slow motion. It seems as if I have all the time in the world to watch the receivers run their patterns and yet I know the defensive line is coming at me just as fast as ever. I know perfectly well how hard and fast those guys are coming, and yet the whole thing seems like a movie or dance in slow motion. It's beautiful.[1]

It is interesting here that modern physicists who, having taken their science to its very limits, to the sub-atomic particle, have, like these sportsmen, found space and time taking on new dimensions and challenging much existing wisdom and theory. For a detailed discussion see Fritjof Capra's book *The Tao of Physics.*

### The Quality of Wholeness in the Peak Moment

For Maslow, 'it is the ability to perceive the whole and to rise above parts which characterizes cognition in the various peak experiences'.[2] In practice this means a state of mind which unites all our many skills and capacities. It means the fusion of left and right brain, in Ornstein's scheme, to create golfing synergy. Awareness must unite with will, emotion, the senses, the physical body and the analytical mind to create the peak sporting performance. This wholeness expresses what it means to have adopted, successfully, a Systems approach to golf. The great service of Maslow and Murphy in particular has been to outline just what is involved in realizing and experiencing this 'wholeness'.

### *Awareness – a Selection of Technique*

As increasing numbers realize how awareness plays a central role in man's various activities and, indeed, in life generally a plethora of techniques and approaches have been evolved. They all, in their individual ways, work toward developing awareness in the human organism. What has also emerged is a clearly defined and growing group of individuals who follow the techniques which are collectively described as the Human Potential Movement or the Growth Movement. A selection of the more significant and relevant of these awareness techniques will now be briefly described. It should, however, be said that what these disparate disciplines endeavour to

[1] G. Leonard *The Ultimate Athlete*, p. 39
[2] A. H. Maslow *Towards a Psychology of Being*, p. 91

create is an *experience*, and, as this is necessarily subjective and unique, it will not and cannot be conveyed in a few words.

### Tai Chi and Aikido

These two Eastern martial arts are basically methods of self-defence, apparently developed to enable Buddhist monks to defend themselves without killing their attackers. Nowadays, especially in the West, Tai Chi and Aikido have become instead methods for developing mind/body harmony through movement. They are, therefore, working towards the Existential Level in the framework of levels of awareness developed earlier – the level characterized by the fusion of mind and body in the task. As disciplines they have much in common with Hatha yoga (Chapter 5). These body disciplines help develop concentration as well as getting the vital life energies flowing again.

### Encounter Groups

Group workshops are intended to create a safe environment in which the individual can take risks and experiment with new forms of behaviour. It is a way of moving your behavioural 'edge' in the way that Hatha yoga takes you to your physical 'edge' (Chapter 5). Because the participants are encouraged to express their feelings honestly and openly, the individual can obtain feedback both positive and negative which he normally would not receive in his day-to-day existence. The group effectively acts as a mirror, enabling the individual to see how others see him and how he comes across.

The relevance to the golfer is that it provides an excellent way of 'taking stock' of his various sub-personalities. This has been explained already as an essential stage in psychosynthesis, the approach which works at the discovery of the true Self, the orchestra's conductor. It might also give hints as to the reasons why other areas of life are not working too well, such as home or work. It is the premise of this book that these 'other areas' play a vital role in what goes on on the golf course.

### Gestalt Therapy

Gestalt therapy is a theory and approach to personality integration. The word 'gestalt' actually means 'whole' or 'total' and it is this that the gestalt therapist or group leader endeavours to develop in the participant. Like encounter, it involves moving to our edge and into the unknown. The emphasis is on bringing the participant into the present moment – the 'here and now'. In doing so, awareness exercises are used which involve the group working together or with each other or even individually with the leader.

The relevance to the golfer of the 'here and now' becomes apparent in the following few words from the founder of Gestalt Therapy, Fritz Perls:

> the formula of anxiety is very simple; anxiety is the gap between the now and the then. If you are in the now, you can't be anxious, because the excitement flows immediately into outgoing spontaneous activity. If you are in the now, you are creative, you are inventive. If you have your senses ready, if you have your eyes and ears open, like every small child, you find a solution.[1]

This truly highlights the problem of so many golfers, they spend their time either in the past or the future and never in the present. They can't think of one shot at a time.

### Bioenergetics

Bioenergetics is based on the work of William Reich and involves working with the body using breathing, moving and the expression of feeling. The theory is that because of our psychological troubles we create 'armouring', or energy blocks, in the body which keep us from living our life to the full. Bioenergetics aim to free these blocks. For the golfer the release of psychosomatic tensions means, as these are held in the muscles, a more flexible body and one better able to use its potential.

### Biofeedback

Biofeedback is an approach to awareness which takes advantage of Western technology. It employs instruments which provide the individual with information about his inner world. Certain biofeedback machines are able to monitor even slight shifts in biological and mental functions. For the golfer, the prospect of being able to teach himself how to control his brain waves, his muscles and the other automatic processes of the body with the help of a machine is an exciting prospect!

### Biorhythms

Biorhythms are the biological cycles that the body goes through. It is possible to buy charts to plot your own particular rhythms and to find out, for example, the best time of the month for intellectual endeavour or the best time for play or competition. While this will not enable you to alter what is happening, even if that were a good idea, it can increase your understanding of why you feel the way you

[1] F. S. Perls *Gestalt Therapy Verbatim*, p. 3

do at certain times of the month, and the more you understand, the better a position you are in to take action.

SUMMARY

The central role occupied by the concept of awareness has become increasingly apparent. This chapter has drawn together the different perspectives on awareness and has put forward some new aspects. Perhaps the most significant point made in the chapter is that a golf shot, in its execution, demands the attention of the faculties of the right side of the brain while the left side is effectively put to rest – and yet our whole educational system stresses and develops the left brain faculties. The techniques outlined in the last part of the chapter attempt to redress this imbalance. It is time they played a more significant part in the total development and training of the golfer.

RECOMMENDED FURTHER READING

1) K. Wilber *The Spectrum of Consciousness*
2) Charles T. Tart *Altered States of Awareness*
3) G. Leonard *The Ultimate Athlete*

Some of the information in this chapter is derived from a lecture given by Tony Buzan on 'Mankind's Potential' at the 1977 Festival for Mind and Body at London's Olympia.

# *Chapter Thirteen*

## THE COMMON CHARACTERISTICS ARGUMENT II

*'You can find golfers of twenty years experience still afraid of the ball. They never know what a shot is going to be like till they can see it, and too often it is not worth seeing.'*

*'. . . my aim is to get the learner or medium player into the right frame of mind, with just one or two rock-bottom principles to guide him, and not a crowd of ideas to bewilder him.'*

One of the main arguments for a Systems approach is that it will reveal characteristics common to all systems no matter how simple or complicated, and that this 'provides a valid and powerful form of generalisation'.[1] The first part of this 'common characteristics' approach to the golfing bodymind dealt with the question of goals, a most important 'abstract' characteristic of the living system (Chapter 9). In this chapter the search for common characteristics will continue with a view to validating the argument put forward by F. E. Emery in *Systems Thinking.* This approach is very different from the traditional emphasis of the scientist who has tended to look for those characteristics of the system that are unique.

There is no doubt that the common characteristics argument can be applied with benefit to the technical, mechanical side of the game. It stresses the importance of getting the 'basics' right. Many good golf teachers repeatedly emphasize this point, as do many of the great players. For example, Jack Nicklaus in *Golf My Way:*

> I believe the best a fellow can do to get himself a good golf game is to select those fundamentals that have been common to the greatest number of good players down the years, then apply them as assiduously as his talent, opportunity and desire allow.[2]

[1] F. E. Emery *Systems Thinking*, p. 7
[2] J. Nicklaus *Golf My Way*, p. 22

This book, however, is not about the technical side of the game so the 'common characteristics' argument will be applied to the golfing bodymind as a whole. Those characteristics found to be common to all living systems will be described in turn and then related to golf.

*Energy Input / Through-Put / Output*

The open living system takes energy from the environment, transforms it and then restores some product into the environment. In the human organism there are three I.T.O processes. One of these is the breathing process which has already been considered at various stages. Another is the eating/drinking/excretion process which will be considered briefly in a later chapter.

The third I.T.O process was first considered when the work of F.M. Alexander was introduced. This is the mental processing which follows the *in*put of some data (internal or external) via one of the senses and results in some *out*put to the environment (again either internal or external). What is so significant about this vision of man's behaviour is that it runs contrary to the prevailing attitude of modern psychology which has been dominated until recently by behaviourism and Freudian psychoanalysis. Behaviourism is based on a concept of stimulus-response (S-R) or in Alexander's language, an I.O sequence. Behaviour, whether animal or human, was thought to be based on a response to external stimuli. Incidentally, many of the behaviourist theories were drawn from experiments which were carried out on animals (notably those of Skinner and Pavlov) and which were not necessarily tested on humans. The other major school was Freudian and saw our behaviour as determined largely by internal stimuli of which the individual was largely 'unconscious' – including tensions, fears and urges as well as a number of drives and instinctual forces.

Neither of these viewpoints are particularly helpful for the golfer since their ultimate view of man is basically of a robot-like system capable only of reacting passively to stimuli. This view implied that man was *not* in control, and was *not* in a position to determine his destiny on the golf course or anywhere else. M. Murray, a leading personality theorist, has the following to say about conventional 'scientific' psychology:

> Man is a computer, an animal, or an infant. His destiny is completely determined by genes, instincts, accidents, early conditionings and reinforcements, cultural and social forces . . . In the majority of our personalogical formulations there are no provisions for creativity, no admitted margins, freedom

> for voluntary decisions, no fitting recognition of the power of ideals . . . If we psychologists were all the time, consciously or unconsciously, intending out of malice to reduce the concept of human nature to its lowest common denominator, and were gloating over our success in doing so, then we might have to admit that to this extent the Satanic spirit was alive within us.[1]

The problem facing psychologists is the difficulty of studying, in a truly scientific manner, that which is most important – man's awareness or consciousness – and a quality unique almost to man. They are unable to be totally 'objective' about something that is not external and visible and they therefore ignore it. The result is a much impoverished discipline which is basically of little use to the golfer. This partly explains why there have been so few books on the psychology of golf, even though it is well recognized to be a 'mental game'. What a terrible pity we ignored Alexander's wise words of some fifty years ago for he understood man in a way we are only beginning to appreciate today.

But we are beginning to appreciate his words because we are studying man's consciousness, his awareness and his will, even if it does mean breaking down the subject-object split which has obsessed the scientific community for so long. In psychology the emergence of the humanistic and transpersonal psychologies, the 'third' and 'fourth' forces, mark this trend. In this book each of the major disciplines or techniques discussed concentrated on the 'T' (the Transformation stage in Alexander's model) – what it means in practical terms is 'conscious control'. If Alexander concentrated on the physical dimension, psychosynthesis established a balance by outlining the mental aspects of 'conscious control': in other words, by considering the vital matter of the human *will.* The Eastern disciplines of yoga and zen have a long tradition in these matters and have, fortunately, been immune to the attempts of Western science to do man an injustice. The conclusion of these various disciplines is that we *can* exert control. For the golfer, this is good news. These Systems views are positive, what is more, they are optimistic.

### *Systems as Cycles of Events*

According to Katz and Kahn:

> The pattern of activities of the energy exchange has a cyclic

[1] M. Murray 'The Personality and Career of Satan', *Journal of Social Issues* 18, 1962

> character. The product exported into the environment furnishes the sources of energy for the repetition of the cycle of activities.[1]

This cyclical pattern has very important implications for the golfer.

At an earlier stage in the book (Chapter 4) it was shown how a negative thinking cycle, developed from the bad shot, or bad performance, tended to lead to a negative thought process which ensured the repetition of that bad shot. This was given as an example of a vicious circle in operation, and it was suggested how the approaches of both positive thinking and psychocybernetics are making a direct attack on different aspects of this all-too-common cycle.

At the other extreme, there is no doubt that positive cycles operate. For example, it is often said 'in' golf that 'success breeds success', and that there is nothing more conducive to a win than a win. This observation recognizes the vitally important role of self-confidence. The problem for many golfers is that it is difficult for them to think positively about the next shot because they hit so many bad ones.

There seem to be three important things which tie up with this cyclical way of life. One is the importance of the zen concept of 'non-judgemental awareness'. In effect this means being aware of what kind of shot you have hit (but not passing judgement on it, particularly if it is bad). Passing negative judgement will merely reinforce a negative cycle. Another point is that as golfers we will all have hit both good and bad shots which we are likely to remember. It is our choice whether it is the good or the bad that we recall. If we wish to get a positive cycle going it must be the good shots that we bring back into consciousness.

The final point to remember, as we have said, is the crucial importance of positive visualizations. A positive visualization will provide the energy for the repetition of the cycle. It all brings to mind Shivas' notion of 'streamers of heart power for the ball to fly on'.[2]

*Negative Entropy*

> To survive open systems must move to arrest the entropic process, they must acquire negative entropy. The entropic

[1] F. E. Emery *Systems Thinking*, p. 93

[2] M. Murphy *Golf in the Kingdom*, p. 80

> process is a universal law of nature in which all forms of organization move towards disorganization and death.[1]

If we as golfers were entirely bound by this law, it would bode ill for the golfer and would seem to imply a natural tendency to 'give up' or 'crack up', especially under the often adverse circumstances that are inevitable on the golf course. What the golfer (as an open system) can do, however, is to import more energy from the environment than he uses and store it. This excess energy can be used to create a higher degree of organization within the system. So, to sum up, the news from science of the open system is again good news. Ludwig von Bertalanffy explains: 'Living systems maintain themselves in a state of high order and improbability, or may even evolve toward increasing differentiation and organization as is the case in organismic development and evolution.'[2]

What this means in simple terms is that there is a process at work in the open system (the human organism) which moves the system towards a state of chaos and disorganization. But this process can be counteracted by acquiring energy from the environment. It is up to the individual to determine whether the process is in the ascendancy or whether he can counteract it sufficiently to move him towards a higher degree of order. Simply maintaining a neutral state of organization is difficult because there are powerful forces in the environment which eventually disrupt what neutrality may have been achieved. We must, then, work continuously to organize our system in a positive direction.

### *Information, Input, Negative Feedback, and the Coding Process*

> The reception of inputs into a system is selective. Not all energic inputs are capable of being absorbed into every system . . . systems can react only to those information signals to which they are attuned.[3]

This applies directly to the golfing bodymind as a living system. The Cambridge philosopher, Dr C. D. Broad says:

> The function of the brain and nervous system is to protect us from being overwhelmed and confused.[4]

[1] F. E. Emery *Systems Thinking*, p. 94
[2] L. von Bertalanffy *General Systems Theory*, p. 150
[3] Katz and Kahn in F. E. Emery *Systems Thinking*, p. 96
[4] Aldous Huxley *The Doors of Perception*

and from Colin Wilson:

> our senses are 'filters' whose main function is to 'keep out' experience rather than letting it in. When a man walks through the streets of a large town, his senses are being bombarded by impressions that would drive him insane if he 'noticed' them all. The healthier a man is, the more he can ignore; it is the unhealthy man whose nerves are torn to shreds every time a baby cries or a door slams. Our senses are 'selective', one neurologist estimated that they 'cut out' about 95% of our possible experience. This explains why human beings find it so easy to distort reality.[1]

These observations help explain how the golfer, who is completely absorbed, can actually *not hear* things (like the train that rattled by Joyce Wethered at Troon just as she was putting) or, conversely, why certain people are continually complaining of distraction on the course. The golfer who comes into the latter category has, without realizing it, actually trained his senses to pick up the camera clicks or the partner's white shoes moving. As he is standing over his putt, he is hyper-sensitive to the possible distractions.

One of the functions of the techniques of concentration so far suggested is to break down the psychological structures that organize, limit and interpret the stimuli received from the outside world. The rationale behind this is that concentration increases our awareness by breaking down our habits of analysing and interpreting all the stimuli we receive through the senses. If we increase our awareness, we can increase the stimuli, or information, we receive. This is why it is said that concentration helps us see things with which we have become familiar as if they were new (Beginner's Mind, Chapter 6). They seem new not because they have changed but because the structures of the mind, with which they are interpreted, have changed. This has exciting possibilities for those whose golf is largely confined to one course.

I have observed that successful people (speaking generally) are the most receptive. They are prepared ιo look at anything that they feel may be of relevance to their goals, but they look in a critical manner and are quick to discard the irrelevant. It is their skill in that that has a great deal to do with their success.

The problem for the less successful, on the other hand, is twofold: an overabundance of information from the environment or a scarcity of information. In golf this means two types of people. The one who listens to so many advisers and reads so many books that he ends up in a complete muddle, knowing everyone else's views but

[1] Colin Wilson *New Pathways in Psychology*, p. 230

having none himself. The other is the stubborn golfer who is simply unreceptive to advice, thinking all along that he knows it all. He lets nothing in and suffers as well.

Systems theorists have highlighted the simple but valuable nature of negative feedback.[1] This characteristic of all open systems was recognized by Murphy who talks of the value of negative thoughts, which in view of the earlier arguments in favour of positive thinking might seem a bit of a contradiction.[2]

Murphy argues, however, that we should learn to listen to the more persistent of our negative thoughts. He refers to one of his own that kept telling him that he was not lining up his putts correctly. The thought persisted and eventually he realized it had a wider meaning. He had been living in an unbalanced way, and working very hard to the extent that his life had become disorganized. That particular game of golf made him aware of the body's self-regulating, or homoeostatic, devices. Golf acted as his teacher.

The point, really, is that we must think more positively about our game, but not to the extent that we are unaware of useful negative feedback or what may have caused errors and mistakes in the past. Many golfers use the negative result to hit themselves over the head. The wise golfer uses the failure as a learning experience. At my Prep School we had an extremely good rugby coach. I recall one game at the start of the season when we had not only played badly but behaved badly. He wrote ten sheets of critical commentary on the match and made us read it! As a result we learned from an experience we would rather have forgotten. After all, in our failures there is surely more material from which to learn than from our successes, if, that is, we take the opportunity.

*Growth/Change/Dynamic Homoeostasis*

'Open systems which survive are characterized by a steady state. A steady state is not motionless or a true equilibrium.'[3] This means that there is no such thing as equilibrium for the open system. We must be prepared to change and adapt as our environment changes. The only equilibrium we can know is dynamic; we must recognize that we are changing from moment to moment – a biological fact.

'We are in constant exchange with the surrounding environment

[1] Katz and Kahn *Common Characteristics of Open Systems*; F.E. Emery *Systems Thinking*, p. 95
[2] M. Murphy *Golf in the Kingdom*, p. 192
[3] F. E. Emery *Systems Thinking*, p. 96

through respiration, eating and elimination. Radioisotope studies have established the fact that our bodies are in a state of continual turnover of materials. We are not the same collection of atoms that we were a year ago.' Bertalanffy summarizes, 'As a result of its metabolism, which is characteristic of every living organism, its components are not the same form from one moment to the next. Living forms are not in being, they are happening.'[1]

That we are in a constant process of change is proven by the scientist. What remains to us is to determine whether this change is in a positive direction and toward our true potential as human beings and as golfers. Failure to change in a positive direction is to give in to the entropic process, that fundamental law of nature, which moves the open system toward a state of disorganization and death. Neurosis is one major symptom of the failure to adapt. We must counteract this entropic process.

This notion of change and adaptation is inherent in the Alexander Principle. For Alexander, our adaptation to environmental changes is faulty because of the poor state and condition of our bodymind. Correct adaptation would, he argued, proceed and do so automatically if we learned the correct use of our 'living system'; and this naturally includes adapting to the rapid environmental fluctuations we all experience during a round of golf, the high spots and the low spots.

While it is one thing to realize intellectually the vital necessity of individual growth or self-development it is quite another to do something about it. As the 1977 Wimbledon winner, Virginia Wade, so rightly points out:

> It take enormous effort and single-mindedness to effect a change in something so profound as your basic self.[2]

Maslow makes the point that the powerful *experiences* of our life, such as tragedies or death, provide the most significant learning experiences, and therefore are those most conducive to individual growth.

Tom Weiskopf, apparently, found the death of his father, to whom he was very close, a profound learning experience which caused a changed outlook and attitude.

Contemporary humanistic psychology also sees *experience* as conducive to growth. Merely reading about it does not really change anything!

[1] A. J. Deilman 'The Meaning of Everything' in R. Ornstein *The Nature of Human Consciousness*, p. 318
[2] *Quest* magazine, January/February 1978

It is interesting to note here that the basic Freudian psychoanalytic model is *not* based on the concept of growth:

> According to Freud it is the supreme tendency of the organism to get rid of tensions and drives and come to rest in a state of equilibrium governed by the 'principal of stability'.[1]

The real problem with the concept of equilibrium, as von Bertalanffy explains, is that only when the human organism moves away from a state of equilibrium is one capable 'of doing work'. We are freed, then, from Freudian style static concepts and left in a position where we can say, with scientific backing, that from the golfing point of view, there can be no higher aspiration than growing toward your golfing potential.

*Differentiation*

'Open systems move in the direction of differentiation and elaboration.'[2] One manifestation of this is Maslow's observation of the idiosyncratic nature of our highest needs and, in particular, the need for self-actualization. Our higher needs can be fulfilled in many ways, through golf, music, art or even in being a parent. It must, however, be in a way that is true to your inner nature. The important point to be made here is that you may find as you get to know yourself in greater depth, that golf is not the means of satisfying your higher need. You may, of course, find that it is. For Virginia Wade, the discovery that tennis was her means of self-fulfilment was a decisive factor in her Wimbledon victory.

*Equifinality*

This final important characteristic is embodied in a principle which states that 'a system can reach the same final stage from different initial conditions and by a variety of paths'.[3] This principle was used earlier in a criticism of that search for the perfect golf swing which has been occupying the mind of many golfing theorists for a number of years (Chapter 2). The principle makes it clear that there is no perfect swing and never will be.

Nor, it must be said, will there ever be a perfect Systems approach to golf. All there ever will be is a best way for you, both from the

[1] L. von Bertalanffy *General Systems Theory,* p. 114
[2] F. E. Emery *Systems Thinking,* p. 99
[3] Ibid. p. 100

technical and Systems point of view. What is more, it is up to you to find it.

SUMMARY

There is no doubt that some of the characteristics discussed in this chapter are difficult to grasp and will be new to many golfers. The two most significant points to be remembered are: the value of negative feedback as a learning experience for the golfer and the central role occupied by the qualities of growth and change.

The common characteristics argument is thus, without doubt, a 'valid and powerful form of generalization'.

RECOMMENDED FURTHER READING

1) An article in F. E. Emery, *Systems Thinking* provides the background for this chapter: D. Katz and R. L. Kahn, 'Common Characteristics of Open Systems'. This article is very much simpler than some of the material in Emery's book, at least for a non-mathematical reader. It is recommended.
2) Sylvan S. Tomkins *Affect, Imagery, and Consciousness* Vol.I
3) Ludvig von Bertalanffy *General Systems Theory*
4) Gordon W. Allport *Becoming – Basic Considerations for a Psychology of Personality*

# *Chapter Fourteen*

## THE ZEN OF GOLF

*'Now there is a right way and a wrong way of playing golf.'*

In recent years there has emerged a number of notable books which highlight important parallels between sport and religion. Certain cultures, such as the Japanese and the ancient Greeks, explored and developed these interconnections but the notion is new to a western world still struggling with the related idea that the body can be a spiritual path.

It is interesting that the suggestion of a sacred dimension to our Western sports and pastimes comes more from the practical application of the contemplative disciplines of the East than from the established Western religions pondering over their declining influence in increasingly secular culture. However, it is important to get the matter in perspective and particularly to understand why commentators such as Murphy and Herrigel are able to see so clearly these important parallels.[1]

To help do so it is proposed to present an argument developed in an article by psychologist Andras Angyal. In a discussion of the overall pattern of personality functioning Angyal isolates two apparently contradictory characteristics:

> Viewed from one of these vantage points, the human being seems to be striving basically to assert and to expand his self-determination. He is an autonomous being, a self-governing entity that asserts itself actively instead of reacting passively like a physical body to the impacts of the surrounding world. . . This tendency – which I have termed 'the trend toward increasing autonomy' expresses itself in spontaneity, self-assertiveness, striving for freedom, and for mastery.

[1] M. Murphy *Golf in the Kingdom*, E. Herrigel *Zen in the Art of Archery*

This tendency is the main concern of the Systems approach to the golfing bodymind, with its emphasis on the golfer becoming 'the independent variable in his relationship within his environment' and its view that the basic regulation of the open system is self-regulation. The whole drift of the argument is towards mastering the actions of the golfing bodymind. This is obviously very different from what is implied by the second important tendency isolated by Angyal.

> Seen from another vantage point, human life reveals a very different basic pattern. . . In this second tendency. . . [the individual] seems rather to surrender himself willingly to seek a home for himself in and *to become an organic part of something that he conceives as greater than himself.* The super individual unit of which one feels a part, may be variously formulated according to one's cultural background and personal understanding. The superordinate whole may be represented for a person by a social unit – family, clan, nation, or by a cause, an ideology or by a meaningfully organized universe. In the realm of aesthetic, social, and moral attitudes this basic human tendency has a central significance. Its clearest manifestation, however, is in the religious attitude and religious experience.[1]

Any attempt to draw attention to the parallels between sport and religion must concentrate principally on how far the particular sport can meet this second tendency, for it is this 'becoming an organic part of something conceived as greater than himself' that forms the basis of all the major spiritual disciplines. Initially one would think that this had very little to do with golf, for where in such a game is there a place for notions involving the surrender of the individual self?

The answer can, I feel, be split into two parts. There are the parallels which involve the means, or, more explicitly, the methods and techniques, but there are also parallels involving the end state to be reached in both the Eastern disciplines and the new Western approaches to sport and life.

### *Parallels Involving the Means*

Common to most spiritual disciplines and particularly those from the East, is an insistence on a high degree of self-control before any attempt is made to proceed to some of the higher spiritual goals.

[1] Quoted in an article by Peter A. Campbell and Edwin M. McMahon in *The Journal of Transpersonal Psychology*, No. 1 pp. 11-12, 1974

The first two of Patanjali's eight limbs of yoga, yama and niyama, or restraint and self-discipline, make it quite clear what is necessary in the early stage of the classical yogic path. The Christian Ten Commandments provides an outline of a similar kind. Self-control and self-discipline are as important to anyone on a spiritual path as they are to the golfer seeking to realize his potential.

It will have become apparent from the earlier argument (Chapter 6) that what is important in golf is the mind and body working in an integrated way. The emphasis was, therefore, on integration firstly at Level II (or the Ego level) and then at Level III (or the Existential level). This involves an awareness of mind *and* body and thus of deeper needs – the true Self. Awareness is essential to the living Systems' qualities of concentration and equanimity and indeed to the attainment of golfing potential.

Now in terms of spiritual development this awareness and Existential integration must also be seen as important. Patanjali's third and fourth limbs, for example, are asana and pranayama. These are correct posture and control of the life force through correct breathing. They are principally the subject of Hatha yoga, the yoga that works towards unity of mind and body. Clearly the early stages of the spiritual path have much in common with what is involved in the development of inner golf. In terms of Angyal's analysis of the personality it is the tendency 'toward increased autonomy' that must initially be fostered and developed. The final steps in both cases ask a great deal from the system and to take these steps needs, as has been said before, 'a solid place to swing from'.

Another significant parallel involves 'letting go' of what stands in the way of further development. In both cases this relates basically to the thinking, doubting ego-mind that prefers the status quo to stepping out into unknown territory. It must be left behind because as we move towards our 'peaks' it seems to act merely as an inhibiting factor. To recall Alexander's theory of evolution (Chapter 3), this is simply a case of replacing the 'T' in input-throughput-output (I.T.O) process (that is exerting 'conscious control') and then letting it go. In terms of Ornstein's two sides of the brain 'letting go' means learning to trust the right hand side of the brain with its intuitive, holistic mode of functioning.

One final connection involving the path is the use of visualization and imagery. Many Eastern spiritual disciples recognize the power of this mental rehearsal work and give it an important place in their training procedures. While there is a marked absence of visualization work in current golf coaching the top stars rarely fail to stress its importance. Recently some reports of scientific studies have shown the significance in sport of systematic visualization. Australian psychologist Alan Richardson reported in *Research Quarterly* his study of the free-throw scores of basketball players. Three groups of students were chosen at random and their scores in free-throwing recorded. None of these students, it should be noted, had practised visualization. The first group practised every day making throws, the second group did no practice and the third group did no practice but mentally rehearsed throwing. The first group had improved 24 per cent compared with a 23 per cent improvement by the visualizers. Furthermore, psychologist Richard Suinn has reported successful results using mental rehearsal with the U.S. ski teams.[1]

These reports are likely to increase the use of visual rehearsal amongst sports people until it becomes a standard practice amongst them as it has long been in the East.

### *Parallels Involving the Ends*

We have already discussed at some length the peak experiences of which we are all capable with their heightened levels of awareness (Chapters 7 and 12). Because the subjective accounts of these altered states revealed so many features that were in harmony with the Systems approach to the golfing bodymind, they were seen as the proper goal or the 'end state' of the approach. Having taken this as the goal it became apparent that awareness had become both the means to the end and the subjective manifestation of that goal.

The significant point about these 'altered states' is that they are similar in many ways to the mystical states of awareness reported by yogis and zen masters. The amazing state of clarity and focus Jacklin talks of in the Lancôme Tournament, the orientation of time and space, the sense of complete unity and fusion, and the perfect, completely satisfying quality of the experience are all features in common with the experiences of the mystics.

Having recognized these parallels, I suggest that what is really being offered is a philosphy for the sportsperson, a framework on which to ground and deepen their sporting experience. It is this that, sadly, is all too often lacking. American footballer John Brodie puts it so well in the following words:

> Football players and athletes generally get into this kind of being or beingness – call it what you will – more often than is generally recognized. But they often lose it after a game or after the season is over. They often don't have a workable philosophy or understanding to support the kind of thing they

[1] Adelaide Bry *Visualization: Directing the Movies of your Mind*, pp. 53–4.

> get into while they are playing. They don't have the words for it. So after a game you see some of them coming down, making fools of themselves sometimes, coming way down in their tone level. But during the game they come way up. A missing ingredient for many people, I guess, is that they don't have a supporting philosophy or discipline for a better life. [1]

So also are the strange psychical powers or 'siddhis' which again are sometimes evident. On the golf course probably the most frequently experienced siddha is 'precognition' when a golfer knows a putt – or even a chip – is going to go in the hole.

Michael Murphy who has become something of an expert on these matters, has had reports from golfers who have had the experience of changing shape and size during the game. Another of these 'psychic' effects is freedom from the ageing process and Murphy cites Sam Snead's famous swing as an example of a golfer whose game remained unaffected by growing older. In *Golf in the Kingdom* he talks also of the 'mingling of the senses' and how Bobby Jones used to hear a melody during the round and blend it to his swing.

It is no wonder then, with deep understanding that Adam [2] could announce during that drunken but very wise discussion of golfing philosophy round the fire at the McNaughtens that: 'Golf is the new yoga of the supermind.' I think I would temper Adam's claim by saying that it *can be* the new yoga of the supermind, but this depends on the approach of the golfer. However, to the extent that the game is seen as a means of developing firstly existential and then cosmic awareness or 'big mind' the parallels run very close indeed. It remains for us to explore them more fully.

[1] M. Murphy and John Brodie 'I Experience a kind of clarity' *Intellectual Digest* Vol. 3, No. 5, pp. 19-22, January 1975
[2] See M. Murphy *Golf in the Kingdom*, p. 49

## RECOMMENDED FURTHER READING


1) K. von Durckheim *The Way of Transformation, Daily Life as a Spiritual Discipline*
2) Sam Keen *To a Dancing God*
3) M. Murphy 'Sport as Yoga' *Journal of Humanistic Psychology* Vol. 17, No. 4, 1977
4) *Journal of Transpersonal Psychology*
5) Robert M. Pirsig *Zen and the Art of Motorcycle Maintainance*
6) Eugen Herrigel *Zen in the Art of Archery*

# *Part Three*

# SOME IMPLICATIONS

# *Chapter Fifteen*

## THE SYSTEMS APPROACH – IMPLICATIONS FOR THE GAME

*'Mr Lang told me of a King of Scotland – one of the Stuarts, I think – who made a law to stop "gowf" because it took the young men away from their bows and arrows. If any King or President tried to put into force such a law today, I'm thinking there would be a fine hullabaloo.'*

If the theoretical considerations of the two previous sections of this book ever achieve any widespread acceptance amongst golfers certain subtle but important changes would take place in the game as we currently know it. The changes would occur because of a re-alignment of our approach to the game in terms of internal rather than external challenges. In this chapter we shall consider some practical implications for the professional game both for the tournament and club professional, and for the amateur game, both for the competitive and social golfer.

### *The Professional Game*

While the Systems approach to golf is relevant no matter what the golfer's standard, there is no doubt that it comes particularly to the fore once the technical side of the game has been mastered. More and more of the top golfers are likely to start seriously developing their 'inner' game of golf. It is the relationship between golfing mind and the golfing body that comprises the great unexplored area of the game, and one can only speculate upon the standards of performance we will see as our top golfers start exploring, assimilating and applying the methods and approaches outlined in this book.

Another probable development is that growing numbers of the world's professional golfers will start seeing their game as the means of inner development. The parallels between the inner game of golf and the Eastern mystical disciplines will start to become apparent and real, and for professional golfers the harmony of mind, body and soul will become not merely the means of reaching their potential, but a philosophy and a way of being and living that the very game itself can help to develop.

There will be a place then in the tented villages at golf tournaments around the world for the advocates of this 'inner' game. At present these 'villages' cater merely for the commercial side of golf and the material needs of the golfer, but the future will see some dramatic changes. It is possible that various organizations and groups will set up stalls from which they can talk to aspirants about their particular emphasis, their methods and their personnel. For those interested in the game's wider dimensions this would facilitate finding out which path is right for them at the moment, which method most appropriate. This searching is so difficult in practice but so essential. There is good reason as well to expect to hear lectures and see demonstrations from experts on the psychological and psychic aspects of the game.

The resounding success of the Festival of Mind and Body, held at London's Olympia for the last few years, indicates that these developments will take place sooner rather than later. These moves will complement, not contradict, the commercial aspects of the game. There will remain as much work to be done on the commercial side; the inner game merely adds another dimension.

### *The Club Professional*

The Systems approach to golf introduces, I feel, certain new and demanding challenges to the club professional. Rather than being just a specialized shop-keeper and teacher of the technical side of golf, the professional of the future will have several other responsibilities to fulfil.

On the teaching side he will have to be capable of instructing on three different levels:

a) *The Technical/partial approach* This is the level that has received almost exclusive attention to date. It will remain extremely important especially in the early stages of a pupil's game. The partial approach has given us much knowledge and insight, especially in the sciences, and, therefore, there is no way this wisdom can be ignored.

b) *The Technical/holistic approach* It is important for the golf professional to be aware of his pupil's swing as a whole and to see it as such. This is vital because defects in one aspect can be compensated for in others, and failure to recognize these interactions can cause the whole to function less efficiently. It seems fair to say that any technical/partial analysis (as in (a) above) will be inadequate unless an attempt is made to integrate the analysis or diagnosis into a technical/holistic framework. Any good teacher of technique will switch between the two levels almost automatically.

c) *The Systems approach* The final level of analysis relates predominantly to the principles outlined in this book. In practical terms it means that the professional faced with someone who swings too fast must consider whether the speed of the swing is simply a reflection of the speed at which the golfer lives the rest of his life. He must adopt Shivas Irons' role and recognize the vital interactions between the man's way of life and his golf and, what is more, must be prepared to confront his pupil, if he finds it appropriate, with his analysis.

It is all a question of getting to the underlying cause of the golfing problem, and as so often these lie in deeper psychological factors the professional of the future must be ready to probe. Failure to isolate the true cause or failure to recognize a golfing problem as a 'Systems' problem often means that the professional is merely treating a symptom which, in the long run, often complicates or compounds the problem.

The ability, then, to teach and think on three levels is the task of the club professional of the future. Level (c) will put the greatest demands and responsibilities upon the teacher. He will be expected at different times to be something of a psychologist, doctor, guru, sociologist, and a Systems theorist. In fact, I believe that schools and universities may well begin to offer courses and qualifications on the psychological/physical/spiritual dimensions of the game. Teaching golf would be seen as demanding as some of the other more established professional vocations. At the moment it is sometimes seen as a fairly easy option, but this will not continue to be so, I feel. The Systems approach highlights several concepts which it is essential that the golfing teacher understands if he is to fulfil his role adequately. At the risk of being somewhat presumptuous in that I have never taught golf, I feel it is worthwhile outlining these concepts. Some have been discussed before but are brought together here.

a) *The Concept of Equifinality* This concept, which was discussed briefly at an earlier stage (Chapter 2) basically states that the same end can be reached by a variety of paths. The implication is that, for the mechanics of the game, there is no *one* method or approach. The teacher must be flexible and prepared to adapt the techniques to the individual concerned – although there are, of course, a few basic principles which should usually be stressed. Even these, however, must at times be relaxed. There are always exceptions to the general rules.

With this concept in mind it becomes clear that the real skill in teaching lies in selecting the method, from the many available, that best suits the pupil, one which enables him to make the best of what the pupil presents him with in the way of raw material. Obviously an elderly businessman will require a different approach from a young schoolchild. With some two thousand books written on techniques, the professional has a great wealth of theory to study and apply. On the Systems side of golf, there is no limit to the areas that are of relevance. It would need a vast library to handle the books of potential relevance once we move into the realms of the inner golfer. Again it is a question of assimilation and intelligent application in the individual case.

b) *The Concept of Self-Regulation* Any Systems teacher, no matter what the subject, must recognize and apply the basic systems maxim 'that the basic regulation of an open system is self-regulation'. The teacher must resist the tendency to make the pupil increasingly dependant and so must give him the tools by which he can help himself. This might be called a 'non-directive' approach.[1]

I had a very good teacher of golfing technique in the South of England with a great talent for after-dinner speaking. He used to emphasize how important it was to be able to help yourself in the middle of the round and to make the slight adjustments to keep the thing going. He adopted a 'non-directive', self-help approach.

c) *Teaching the Means-Whereby* It is also very important for the teacher to understand Alexander's concepts of 'end-gaining' and the 'means-whereby'. The pupil, for example, may be trying very hard to hit a good shot for the teacher (end-gaining) but the straining and tension that results tends to make it more difficult which leads to further tensions and further failure.

The teacher must learn to recognize the 'end-gaining' process at work, perhaps explain it to the pupil, and emphasize the importance of the 'means-whereby' the successful shot is hit. Alexander placed more emphasis on the process of attaining the goal than on the goal itself.

[1] David Brandon *Zen in the Art of Helping* p. 89

d) *What Is Right Often Feels Wrong* One of the very real problems for the golf teacher lies in the fact that what is *right* from a technical point of view often feels *wrong* to the pupil. Alexander highlighted the inaccurate sensory appreciation that is characteristic of modern man, and showed that we have developed psycho-physical habits which are faulty but which come to feel comfortable. We can reach a stage where we are unable to help ourselves.

Overcoming this particular problem needs a skilled teacher who is able to win the trust of the pupil, for the latter must learn to live with what initially feels unnatural to him. This concept incidentally, applies equally to the mental and emotional side of golf.

e) *All Errors/Faults Are Technical* As all golf theories concentrate on technique there is a natural tendency to think that all golfing errors or faults are technical, hence the person who slices because he has lifted his head because he is not concentrating because of his domestic problems will tend to be given advice about grip or stance. This book, I trust, has suggested that this faulty diagnosis and treatment need not continue.

f) *I May Not Be the Right Teacher!* The concept of equifinality highlights that there may be several paths to the same goal. Teachers of the Systems approach tend to become expert on one or other of these paths. So if it is apparent that pupil or client ought really to be following another path it becomes important for the teacher to swallow his pride and say that really, he does not feel he can help but such-and-such a teacher can act as a guide. This, of course, is far from easy.

g) *Review/Preview* It is my belief that the state of mind which the golfer brings to the first tee determines to a very large extent the degree to which he plays to his potential. In spite of this very little heed is paid in golfing instruction to the value of preparation, particularly mental preparation. The golf instructor in the future is likely to be asked for pre-match instruction on relaxation and visualization techniques.

Likewise the review of rounds in a constructive manner after completion is an area on which the majority of golfers are extremely lax. The only reviewing that seems popular is the rather boring hole by hole commentary in the bar. A serious review on the other hand would involve the maintenance of a journal in which various significant matters whether of a technical or psychological nature were recorded. Journal keeping, incidentally, is a central technique in Assagioli's psychosynthesis. It could also involve the technique of itemized review (Appendix I).

h) *Simulating Pressure Situations* One of the basic arguments of this book is that there is a great deal that can be done by the golfer to develop his ability to handle the crisis situations in competitive golf. Much can be done, however, in practice to simulate the high pressure situation so testing the golfer's ability to stand or fall. For example, holding a putting competition for high stakes in which perhaps ten other club members are doing all in their power (verbally) to put the performer off.

It is interesting that the deliberate use of consciously contrived difficult situations in order to develop or unify are popular in Japanese spiritual disciplines.[1] In one tradition that is spreading in the West, Oki Yoga, the Japanese master is reported to use these methods extensively in his training.

i) *The Concept of 'Being' Intelligence* 'Being' Intelligence is intelligence that results from experience. Knowledge, facts, and theories for example, can be acquired from books and teachers, but this is very different from the type of knowledge that results from having actually experienced something, having lived through it and, most important, learnt from it. The Japanese have two words for experience: KEIKEN and TEIKEN. The one means experience from which something is learnt (experience experience) and the other an experience from which nothing is learnt (experience).

The teacher using 'being intelligence' principles is always going to be more effective than someone merely expounding the untried theories of others. This is particularly the case on the Systems side of golf.

These various points all imply in their different ways that the Systems teachers of the future must be prepared to study their own lives as well as their own golf games in a serious and critical manner. They must be prepared to experiment, take risks and move into the new areas themselves. To do so will be to appreciate the real difficulties of making any true progress in golf. It will also mean that the teacher understands that he is on the 'path' in the same way as his pupil. The teacher/pupil dichotomy will begin to dissolve, as the many interconnections between golf and life become more apparent and, I believe, there will be potential roles of a completely different sort for the club professional. This will become apparent as the primary golfing institution, the golf club, starts to adopt a holistic approach to the golfer, recognizing his many other possible skills and potentials. More of this, however, in the next chapter.

[1] Masahiro Oki *Meditation Yoga* p. 109

*The Amateur Golfer*

The amateur golfer will be faced with a choice. He can choose between playing golf as he always has done (i.e. for competitive, status or social motivations) or he can choose to play the game more for reasons of inner fulfilment and development. I see more and more opting for the latter and being prepared to take the risks and move to whatever their 'edge' might be. While the internal aspects of golf certainly involve moving to the individual's edge, they also necessarily mean the excitement of moving into what is beyond.

With regard to competitive aspects of golf I feel it is worth discussing two tournaments which are held each year on the West Coast of Ireland, for they offer much that is in harmony with the principles of a Systems approach to golf. The events are the South of Ireland and the West of Ireland and they take place on two golf courses amidst scenery that can only be described as majestic. The courses are named after two small villages: Lahinch and Rosses Point. The features that I shall isolate go a long way to defining what I personally would see as being the perfect golf tournament for amateur golfers. They are as follows:

a) *A golf course that is close to nature* Both Lahinch and Rosses Point are seaside courses – 'links' – designed to take advantage of the natural terrain to provide a tough test of golf. They are so close to nature that you sometimes get the feeling that it is not just golf that is asking you what you are made of. The West of Ireland was played this year in a force ten Atlantic gale, with vertical hail stones to contend with, and still the game went on! Looking out to sea it really is, 'next step, New York'.

b) *A contest of match play* This form of golf is surely the real test of character and the game for the amateur. The 'crises' that match play can create are so real, so final. In addition, the opponent is there face-to-face and every shot can potentially change the whole course of the proceedings in a way that is rarely the case in stroke-play.

c) *A carnival atmosphere* The atmosphere at Lahinch and Rosses Point building up to and during the events, seems to pervade the air, to pervade everything. There is a pounding of the heart and a great feeling of anticipation and excitement as you drive up to the course. Supporters come from far and wide whether or not, it seems, they know anything about golf, and surely it is this sense of excitement that makes their trip worthwhile.

d) *Enthusiastic and knowledgeable spectators* The large and enthusiastic galleries are an integral part of the event. They all seem to know everything about all the golfers. A match is not just a game of A versus B but perhaps a Cork man versus a Sligo man, or city versus country (Jackeen versus Culshee), or Protestant versus Catholic, farmer versus business, nice guy versus not-so-nice guy, rebel versus straight, well dressed versus scruffy, good swing versus effective swing, rich versus poor, up-and-coming versus established. Because the spectators know these details each match has an added richness often lacking in the professional game. A victory is a victory not just for the golfer but for his part of the country, for his way of life. Each game has many dimensions.

In addition, the event has a history and matches that were played in the past provide old scores to settle, and these details are not lost to the crowd. In fact, matches seem to stay in the memory and provide talking points for years to come. They certainly provide the material for much good discussion in the evening.

e) *Everyone's a winner* Win or lose everyone seems to enjoy themselves. It seems to be a quality of the Irish that they know how to have fun. The bars and hotels, particularly at Lahinch, fill with golfers singing away their sorrows into the early hours. In fact, it is almost a problem to be playing well because it means early nights and missing out on the fun.

It is a great pity, then, that so many other parts of the golfing world have forgotten how to sing together, for it is a social occasion that seems to bring people together. Too much of our social life seems to be more about splitting up, pairing off. No wonder sociologists and psychologists talk of alienation and anomie in the Western world. We must learn to be together as well as apart. The singing in Ireland reflects this for it switches from solo to chorus, but all the time the whole occasion, the atmosphere, is something more than the individuals and it thus caters for our basic tendency to be part of something greater than ourselves.

f) *The game's the 'thing'* The talk of the singing and dancing gives the impression, perhaps, that the golf becomes of secondary importance. Not so; the attitude is more akin to that described by some words of Andra Kirkaldy some fifty years ago: 'There was a good deal of playing for the glory of winning and then sharing the spoil, or spending it in the good old fashioned style, long before Pussyfoot put his foot in Scotland.'[1]

The impression, too, is that the game is to be thanked as it were,

[1] Andra Kirkaldy *My 50 years of Golf – Memoirs*

for the enjoyment and happiness, and that the singing is almost a song of thanks to golf.

There is another aspect of the competitive amateur game in Ireland that, in the context of the argument, warrants discussion. Each year, every golf club in Ireland participates in a national scratch knock-out competition. To be more precise they participate in both a singles competition (teams of five) and a foursomes competition (two foursomes). The country is divided into four regions; each region runs a knock-out competition to produce a winner who then goes through to the national finals. The competition is always keen, and inevitably every year there are some remarkable results. The events seem to bring the best out of certain people who perhaps would not shine if playing for themselves. The clubs with strong team spirit always seem to produce the best results.

Speaking broadly, the event certainly seems to have the effect of unifying the particular clubs involved. It gives the club a real centre on which to focus and the tremendous interest in the proceedings. Clubs reaching the finals sometimes have as many as 200 of their members travelling to give support. The pressure on the players is, of course, immense, because they have to live with the consequences of their actions perhaps for years, for the occasion will be one of the really significant features of the club's activities in the year: the individual carries the hopes and aspirations of his club and even his whole township. It is a tremendous responsibility, and yet, in true Irish spirit, win or lose, everyone enjoys themselves.

The commendable thing about this particular competition is that it counters the over-emphasis in the golfing world on individual achievement rather than group achievements. A team competition is obviously less selfish, less alienating, and seems able to cater at the same time for two diverse aspects of our personality isolated by Angyal. The team member is at the same moment an autonomous self-governing being, and yet a part of something greater than himself – the team. In addition, in the sense that the competition is on a club level, it is more amenable to the average golfer than the team competition that operates on a national level. It also provides an important focus for our basic golfing institution, the golf club.[1]

[1] It must be said that other parts of the golfing world run inter-club competitions but they seem to lack the sense of occasion that is created in Irish golf.

*The Club Golfer's Game*

Club competitions lack the atmosphere that can be generated, say, in a professional tournament. This is a pity, for the pressure that would be generated would perhaps act as the catalyst for the higher states of awareness that are possible, as we have seen, on the golf course, and would help bring out the best in the club golfer. It would be nice to see the final rounds of the club knock-out competition watched by perhaps a hundred of the club's members. And if it was an auction or sweep that helped to bring them all out, perhaps the money could all be spent in 'the good old fashioned style'.

If the golf was not of a professional standard perhaps the fact that both the participants and their various strengths and weaknesses were well known would add the personal touch. In addition most of the members would have competed and would therefore feel that they had contributed to the occasion.

I feel then that increased support for the club competitions is one move likely to result from the Systems approach to golf. It will occur because the members will become more interested in the whole than the parts – more interested in the club and its well-being than simply themselves. Such a move would give the members a real interest in improving their golf, the standard of the game would improve and it would tend towards an added and healthy cohesion for the club.

# *Chapter Sixteen*

## THE SYSTEMS APPROACH – IN THE CLUBHOUSE

*'So you see golf is not only an old man's game. It is also an old woman's game. We can almost play golf as long as we can see and walk.'*

The interrelationships between the golfing mind and the golfing body have been discussed in this book at some length. The fact that we as a culture have a tendency to adopt an unbalanced approach in the development of certain of our mental faculties has also been noted and considered. What is important is that these aspects of the golfing system on a micro-level have implications on a macro-level – affecting those institutions of which we are a part. This interrelationship between the human system and his institutions is noted by Ken Dychtwald:

> Here in the West, we have chosen to make a duality of the bodymind, separating it into two parts: the psyche, which is considered to live somewhere in the skull between the eyes; and the body, which lives and moves beneath it. This mind/body dualism is reflected in all our institutions and cultural processes. By intellectually dividing ourselves into parts, we encourage intensive specialization and differentiation in all our activities, thereby further encouraging mind/body separation rather than holism.[1]

What has happened is that because of our dualistic approach, we have institutions for work and institutions for play, we have those which concentrate on using our mental faculties and those which use our physical faculties. While in some ways this is inevitable, and indeed desirable, unfortunately this over-emphasis and imbalance fails to recognize vital interactions between mind and body that are vital *whatever* the activity.

[1] K. Dychtwald *Bodymind*, pp. 24-5

This chapter will investigate the likely changes as we move to resolve this fundamental institutional dichotomy that is as evident in our golf clubs as our business and academic institutions. At the same time, I shall indicate what may happen as we start to recognize more fully the golfer's hierachical needs and in particular the higher 'self-actualizing' needs.

This will be done by looking at the golfer as an integrated whole from the viewpoint of the inner game of golf and then considering some other, non-golfing, ways in which the whole golfer could be recognized and catered for.

## Recognizing the Whole – for Golf

The golf club, through its professional, tends to provide satisfactorily for all the external aspects of the game including the provision of equipment, caddies, caddy-cars, as well as advice on that equipment. The professional also gives coaching on the mechanics of the game for the club members. At no stage, however, is any attempt made to facilitate the development of the internal aspects of the game.

When, and if, this imbalance is rectified a large and varied range of activities could be offered by the golf club. Indeed the wise Shivas Irons, the golfing professional who understood the 'inner' golfer, offered group therapy, meditation, and 'golf in true gravity' to the members of Buningbush.[1] Carrying on in this vein there is no reason why yoga or aikido sessions could not become regular activities on the curriculum of the golf club. Furthermore, the local 'Systems' professional could make regular visits to take seminars on the Alexander Technique or the use of mental imagery. Indeed many of the club's members, the doctors and psychologists, are likely to have information of interest to the golfer involved in the inner game.

Visiting lecturers, experts in psychosynthesis, Zen Buddhism or different aspects of yoga, could vary the programme. The more 'intellectual' members of the club might like to meet regularly for discussions or debates on the latest papers on the psychology of golf. In fact, I can even imagine a two-day seminar on perhaps a few pages of what must become the Golfer's Bible – *Golf in the Kingdom.* For those who preferred the physical approach, 'zen-like' runs around the course could become a regular feature. The club's committee meetings could provide long and heated discussions as to whether the club was to invest in a biofeedback machine or a new tractor, or whether remaining funds were to be spent on new books for the club's library or expenses for a visiting lecturer!

[1] M. Murphy *Golf in the Kingdom*, p. 199

The combination of activities might provide a balance between those activities which involved both the right and left hand side of the brain, the thinking and the feeling body. However, recognizing the current societal imbalance, the emphasis would initially be on the feeling/awareness aspects of the bodymind and on the RHS of the brain.

Recognizing the Whole – in other ways.
One of the important characteristics of the needs for self-actualization is their idiosyncratic nature. In Maslow's words:

> The specific form that these needs will take will vary greatly from person to person. In one individual it may take the form of desire to be an ideal mother, in another it may be expressed athletically, and in still another it may be expressed in painting pictures or in inventions. At this level, individual differences are greatest.[1]

Thus not all the members of the golf club will wish to fulfil themselves as golfers, seeing golf as merely complementary to other activities of greater personal importance. There is no reason, however, why the golf club could not offer opportunities for its members to express their potential in other ways. I have come across a couple of examples of clubs already doing this.

One of these is in Ireland concerning a remarkable, larger-than-life, character who spent half the year on cruises entertaining wealthy American tourists, who got married having won a small fortune at a game of poker and who, incidentally, went round a par 70 course in a record 63 after a night on the town. Anyway, one winter he organized the acting talent in his club to put on a comedy show, which included songs and charades making fun of members of the club. Apparently it was a tremendous success, both at the home club and at other clubs in the locality.

Another club where I now live in Bristol, England put on a show for its members, which was also a great hit within the club. This time another acting character, an ex-Black and White Minstrel, involved three of the club's low handicap golfers in the proceedings. It would seem that the confidence that results from being a good golfer gives a man the courage to let his hair down in public. We might start finding all sorts of hidden talent in our golf clubs, musicians, singers and song-writers. It is simply tragic that so much of this sort of talent remains dormant and undiscovered.

[1] A. H. Maslow *Motivation and Personality*, p. 46

Another 'forgotten' art is that of speaking. What about debates on sporting, social, political or economic issues similar to those held in Universities? And what about story-telling? As Ornstein reminds us:

> The story-teller is a person who has largely gone out of our culture. Yet in cultures of the Middle East and Central Asia, he remains in a special place. When we read, we usually do it silently and visually, but when a story is read aloud other possibilities emerge. We have more time to imagine the events, and this imagining is aided by the fact that our eyes and visual systems are not involved in the printed page.[1]

I remember my days at Trinity College, Dublin when we used to play golf at Portmanock. After a tough round on a wintry day we would end up round the fire eating toasted bacon and egg sandwiches and scones. Harry Bradshaw (who lost an Open when his ball finished in a bottle) would sometimes come in and tell stories. He could go on for hours and it didn't matter that sometimes you heard the stories twice. It was the way they were told that was important.

And dancing? I remember an old old lady called Julie Maguire, who used to let us stay on her land when we went fishing, on a mountain lake in South West Ireland. Julie had spent fifty years in America as a nurse before returning to marry her childhood sweetheart and she used to talk about how they used to meet at the crossroads when she was a young girl to dance. Why don't we dig up some of these old dances, and develop some more of our own and dance them to celebrate the joy of being alive like they did eighty or ninety years ago in Ireland?

### *The Importance of Participating*

One of the characteristics of all the above activities is that they involve participating and involvement from the individual. This, of course, is in marked contradistinction to so much of the entertainment we have on offer. Television, for example, demands a completely passive audience in which, apparently, not even the eyes have to move! Cinema and radio have a similar effect: such entertainment is *too* accessible. This point, however, is that only by getting involved can the golfer learn about his 'edge' and beyond, which means giving as well as receiving.

The type of entertainment we can expect in the future in our golf

[1] R. Ornstein *The Psychology of Consciousness*

clubs would have much in common with an event popular in rural Ireland called a ceilidh (pronounced kaley). At a ceilidh everyone is involved and anyone who wishes makes a contribution to the occasion whether it be reciting a poem, singing a song or telling a story. There are events which involve everyone and others are for the individual.

The main aspect though is the singing and dancing. Important to the occasion is the involvement and, in the case of the individual's contribution, it matters not whether it is good or bad; the main thing is the act of contributing which is appreciated and respected by the group as a whole.

Nor does it matter whether you are old or young, rich or poor, city or country, pretty or not so pretty, clever or dull. The occasion seems to break down these meaningless dualisms in order to bring people together.

### Recognizing Old Age

We will all be faced sooner or later with our old age, so when considering the 'whole' it is an aspect that cannot be ignored. Robert De Ropp splits life from conception to death into four sections. The first phase lasts nine months, and is the spell from conception to birth. The second lasts from birth to puberty. The third from puberty to approximately the fiftieth year and the final phase from the fiftieth year to death. In our culture this last phase can prove to be a harrowing or frightening period in which the individual feels very alone, perhaps resenting his being ignored after a lifetime of valuable service to the community.

It need not be like this. As De Ropp points out, it is possible to approach this 'phase of life with eagerness and pleasure', provided, that is, that the individual has guarded his 'inner resources' during the earlier phase of life. There seems to be two things of importance to be said here. One is that the arguments and techniques of this book concern the development of the golfer's 'inner resources' with a view to the attainment of that golfer's full potential. The same resources are going to be of value in old age.

The other point is that these resources often take a long time to develop, and frequently it will be the old that have the time, experience and knowledge, to be able to develop, acquire and finally teach the fruits of a lifetime of study. When we start to talk of our inner life perhaps the old can offer the greatest wisdom. In this context, the golf club could become a centre from which to develop fully during the final phase of life. It could also give an opportunity for the young to benefit from the inner wisdom of the senior citizen, providing an important area in which the young could recognize and value the older members of the club. As Christiansen points out: 'A crucial support for dignity with ageing . . . is social recognition commensurate with the ability and powers the ageing person retains.'[1]

My hopes have been well summarized by the anthropologist Margaret Mead who spent her career studying different societies and cultures. Mead 'envisions the planning of small and dependent communities, larger than the family and smaller than the city, where the ties between the generations can be nourished, human satisfactions again known, and where urban opportunities for diversity and development can be had near natural settings.[2]

It seems to me that the golf club is the ideal community for making Mead's vision a reality. It poses quite a challenge!

[1] Drew Christiansen 'Dignity in Ageing', *Journal of Humanistic Psychology*, Vol. 18, No. 2, 1978

[2] Jean Houston discussing M. Mead in an article 'Re-seeding America' in the *Journal of Humanistic Psychology* Vol. 18, No. 1, 1978

## RECOMMENDED FURTHER READING

1) Drew Christiansen 'Dignity in Ageing: Notes on Geriatric Ethics' *Journal of Humanistic Psychology* Vol. 18, No. 2; 1978
2) Robert De Ropp *The Master Game*
3) Frederick Rohe *The Zen of Running*
4) Jean Houston 'Re-seeding America' *Journal of Humanistic Psychology*, Vol. 18, No. 1, 1978

# *Chapter Seventeen*

## THE SYSTEMS APPROACH – OFF THE COURSE

*Presently a bird began singing in the tree, and Mr Balfour lifted his head and remarked, in deep, musical tones, to the amusement of all his audience, 'How sweetly that throstle sings'.*

*'Davie, I was very glad to see you at the prayer meeting last night.' 'O, that's whar I got tae, was it?' said Davie.*

Many golfers would, perhaps justifiably, argue that the real obstacle to reaching their golfing potential was the limited amount of time they had to spend at the game. How can I play my best golf, they argue, when I have a responsible job and a family to attend to which limit the time I can spend to one or two games a week?

While these other responsibilities are inevitable, what the golfer *can* attempt is to reach his potential *within* the constraints he finds himself. This at least would amount to a considerably more positive attitude. Those vital internal Systems qualities, that have been isolated as essential facets which must be developed if the golfer is to reach his potential, are also qualities that are essential for success in every walk of life. Concentration, equanimity and awareness are as vital to the golfer as they are to the musician, doctor or accountant. Indeed, they are the 'means-whereby' whatever the activity or pastime.

Tony Buzan distinguishes between traditional education and progressive education. In the former, he argues, the flow of information is from the subject (whether mathematics, history, philosophy or the technical approach to golf) to the individual, who is supposed to absorb and remember as much as possible. Progressive education, on the other hand, teaches the individual the 'means-whereby' he can learn and the 'means-whereby' he can tackle the many and varied problems which life throws at him –

whether academically, socially or on the golf course. The emphasis is, therefore, on teaching the individual about feeling, thinking, learning, sensing, perceiving, moving, and creating.

The emphasis adopted in this book is of the latter type, as are all Systems approaches to problems, because it is the Systems approach that gets down to basics (Chapter 13), stressing that it is those, first and foremost, that the system must put in order. Thus, it is not entirely valid for the golfer to argue that his other responsibilities detract from his reaching his full golfing potential, for if he adopts a Systems approach he will ensure that in fulfilling the other facets of his life he is developing the qualities or 'means' that are so essential on the golf course.

### *Looking Critically at Other Aspects of Life*

If the golfer accepts this argument, it follows that he must start to look critically at those various other aspects of his life. He must look critically for he may not be taking the opportunity to develop the vital 'means' while at home or at work.

Another reason why he must look critically is because often it may be non-golfing aspects that are the underlying cause of golfing problems. The best example is, of course, the golfer who rushes around like a madman all week and then swings like a madman on the course.

### *Learning to Say 'Yes' – Overshoot and False Start*

Most of the methods so far discussed are very good at teaching us to say 'no'. The Alexander Technique teaches us to 'inhibit' our response to environmental stimuli. Both yoga and zen are extremely strict disciplines which, while recognizing that the ultimate aim is to learn to say 'yes', or in Murphy's words 'collapsing with grace under that pressure from within',[1] stress and teach a way that involves saying 'no'.

The problem is that too many 'no's' and we forget how to say 'yes'. I wrote an essay for a competition run by an accountancy magazine suggesting that the reason that accountants were so often the people to put the dampers on the entrepreneurs' schemes and ideas was that they had spent so long suppressing their desire to go out and enjoy themselves while studying for exams, that when the

[1] M. Murphy *Golf in the Kingdom*, p. 196

time came in business to say 'yes' they no longer knew how. I also suggested that perhaps they spend so much time in the LHS of their brains that they do not have the entrepreneurs' imagination which could see the scheme working. Nor do they tend to share the 'gut feel' of the entrepreneur. Both feeling and imagination, it will be recalled, are associated with the RHS of the brain.

There are times when it is right to say 'yes'. A friend had been working hard at his golf for the British Youths a few years ago, but ended up with a very disappointing first round. The best remedy, he decided, was a 'good few ales'. Indeed it was, for the next two rounds were 65's – course records, 12-under par and he ended up the winner. Jack Nicklaus, I believe, applied the same method at the British Open at Troon – and went out in the final round to break the course record with a 66. Letting the hair down now and then seems to cleanse, refresh and creates a greater state of balance. And, more often than not, it is our own bodies that will tell us when to do so. If we would only listen!

In Systems theory these suggestions of occasionally 'letting the hair down' would be explained by a phenomenon known as *false start*. This is where a system initially moves in a direction contrary to that which leads to a steady state.

Not surprisingly, Shivas understood the value of the false start.

'Tae enjoy yersel', tha's the thing, and beware the quicksands of perfection.'[1] As Murphy so rightly points out, it is all too easy to become fanatical about these ideas of self-improvement, or worse still, to adopt a ' "holier than thou" attitude'.

Moving away from a steady state also occurs with a golfer who is trying too hard to succeed. In this case the phenomenon is called *overshoot* by the Systems theorist.

### *Miscellaneous 'Off the Course' Matters*

No discussion these days, it would seem would be complete without considering the subjects of sex and diet and I certainly don't propose to pass them by.

#### Sex

On reading several experts' opinions of this interesting topic it seems there may be certain aspects in contemporary wisdom of relevance to the golfer. Here I shall consider briefly the work of two of these experts with a view to highlighting the parallels between sex and the

[1] M. Murphy *Golf in the Kingdom*, p. 177

Systems approach to golf.

One of these is the controversial Wilhelm Reich who has done some useful work on the subject of psychosomatic tension and on character armour. His work is considered by Ken Dychtwald in his book *Bodymind*.

> The healthy person, according to Reich, was the one who regularly engaged in lovingly uninhibited sexual exchange leading to a thoroughly satisfying orgasm. The unhealthy person, on the other hand, because of neurotic symptoms and rigid character traits, was unable to give himself fully to the intensity of the sexual encounter and was, as a result, unable to experience a full orgasm and a full release of sexual energy. In fact, Reich postulated that all neurotic symptoms were in some way tied up in to damned up sexual energy.[1]

The main point of relevance here is the concept of 'letting go' in the sexual situation. 'Letting go' was earlier explained as being central to zen and yoga (the concept of detachment), it is also implied by the Alexander Technique in the suggested return to the first stage of our evolution. 'Letting go' was seen as the prerequisite of those peak moments on the golf course. It is all a case, in sex and in golf, of trusting our biological nature.

Another parallel emerges in De Ropp's *The Master Game.* De Ropp like Rollo May[2], is heavily critical of our obsessions with sexual techniques and demands a return to the spiritual and emotional side of sex:

> In our culture sex has become more and more cerebral. We think about it, write about it, talk about it, cold-eyed sexologists gather statistics about it, so that the whole sexual mechanism becomes permeated with verbalizing. This, plus the residue of guilt and shame that, despite more enlightened attitudes, continue to haunt us, puts pure sexual experience out of reach of many people. They simply cannot let the sexual center alone . . . [3]

This plea has much in common with the earlier argument for the Systems, 'holistic' approach to golf to offset our current over-emphasis on technique. Sex, like golf, is an activity which involves the RHS of the brain but we have made it increasingly a LHS activity. Too much thinking is as harmful in bed as it is on the golf course!

One final important parallel is the belief that both sex and golf can be paths to spiritual enlightenment. The golfing path has

[1] Ken Dychtwald *Bodymind*

[2] See Rollo May *Love and Will*

[3] Robert S De Ropp *The Master Game*, p. 156

already been discussed at some length (in Chapter 14) and, indeed, excellently outlined by Michael Murphy. The path to enlightenment through sexual involvement is at the basis of certain branches of Eastern spiritual disciplines. One of these is Tantric yoga:

> Within the vast and somewhat mysterious field of Tantric yoga, it is believed that sexuality can be a wondrous vehicle for increased self-awareness and heightened consciousness. According to William Irwin Thompson, 'The Tantrics maintain that there is enormous energy locked into sexuality, which, if released from the lower end of the spine, can flow up the spinal column to bring divine illumination to the brain'.[1]

Knowing the contemporary attitude of the Christian Church, especially in Catholicism, many are likely to find these ideas somewhat outrageous. All Systems theory can say is that (as we have seen) the same end can be reached by a variety of paths.

There is another important dimension of this concept of sex and sexuality. Our Western world had tended to be polarized into male and female. There have been jobs for men and jobs for women (usually less skilled and less demanding) and ways of life for men and for women. Western society has been predominantly male-oriented.

The emergence of the Women's Rights Movement, however, has been a concerted attempt to tackle this powerful dualism. If the Women's Rights is a plea from women for the masculine part of them to be given equal recognition with the feminine, it should encourage the Western man to start looking for the feminine part in him, for this is what he will have to do if he is ever to reach his potential. The East teaches that we have in us male energies (Yang forces) and female energies (Yin forces) and we must work towards harmonizing these energies. The Eastern symbol of the Yin and the Yang shown below is a representation of this idea which all ties up with Ornstein's conceptions of the LHS and RHS of the brain.

*The Symbol for the Harmony of the Yin and Yang*

| YANG | YIN |
|---|---|
| Masculine | Feminine |
| LHS | RHS |
| Analytical | Holistic |
| Intellectual | Intuitive |
| Active | Receptive |
| Right side of body | Left side of body |
| Technique | Systems |

[1] K. Dychtwald *Bodymind*, p. 110

The LHS in Eastern philosophy would represent the Yang or masculine energies. Golf demands, at its highest levels, qualities normally associated with the RHS or feminine energies, such as images and feelings. In this regard the task for the Western male golfer becomes one of realizing and developing the Yin or feminine within him; consequently, this raises the need to modify the male aspect – forcing, striving and aggression. One is reminded of some words from the sacred Taoist *Tao Te Ching:* 'The best charioteers do not rush ahead, the best fighters do not make displays of wrath, the greatest conquerer wins without joining issue'.[1]

The female golfer will tend to have to work in the opposite direction – developing male qualities. It may need the male impetus to strive for the completion of any meaningful task and to enable the system's potential to be realized. Also, there are times on the golf course when it is very necessary to be 'masculine'. However, the female golfer need not feel threatened by this for it does not mean the abandonment of feminine characteristics. What we are after is harmony.[2]

## Diet

A friend of mine does not like to eat before tournament rounds. He likes to induce a state of physical hunger as a prerequisite to the hunger to do well and develop the 'killer instinct' that can be helpful in the competitive situation. Whatever the reason, it is important to determine what is right for you. This would be in line with the Systems concept of 'self-regulation'. I personally find that a big lunch makes me very sluggish and that raw onions in the salad stay with me all afternoon – but everybody's different.

As regards the most suitable type of food to eat, Systems thinking would go along with the current movement towards 'whole' foods. In practice this means eating unrefined foods and increasing the fibre content of the diet – wholemeal bread, bran, raw fruit and vegetables, etc. At a lecture in London Dr Barbara Latto quoted studies which showed that the intestinal transit time (the time taken for food to pass through the system) varied greatly between different peoples. While an African on an unrefined diet had a transit time of 35 hours, British people on a refined diet had a transit time of 77 hours. This increased time meant a greater frequency of obesity, gall-stones, varicose veins, and cancer of the bowel and, of course, constipation. Denis Burkitt, a Senior Research Fellow at St Thomas's Hospital, London, goes so far as to suggest that many of

[1] Translation taken from A Waley *The Way and its Power*, p. 227

[2] See J. Singer *Androgyny*, for an excellent discussion of these points.

the ills of Western civilization become apparent from a glance at the modern lavatory with its mini library and in certain cases, telephones. There is even, according to Mr Burkitt, a perfect human stool!

Whatever the future, let us hope golf clubs like Rye and Muirfield continue with their superb golfer's lunches, even if they do swop the brown rolls for white. There can surely be no finer feeling than setting out for a tough day's golf on a brisk spring day on these great seaside courses with the thought of the lunch to follow, and another round, no doubt aided by a few glasses of port or brandy.

## SUMMARY

For many golfers the direction of this book may seem somewhat self-indulgent, the whole emphasis is on our internal worlds and our inner conflicts, with the clear implication that this is where we must concentrate in order to reach our true potential. What is more it has been suggested that this inner search should be conducted both on the course and away from it.

While initially it may appear this way, I am more inclined to go along with a view expressed recently by an ever-increasing number of writers and singers, the view that it is now time to attend to this inner search for we have conquered to a large extent, so many aspects of the world about us. This is the message communicated by American singer Tom Paxton when he sings, 'Peace will come, let it begin with me' and by Robert Pirsig in his best-selling *Zen and the Art of Motorcycle Maintenance* when he says 'social values are right only when individual values are right. The place to improve the world is first in one's own heart and head and hands and then work outward from there.'[1] It is also Ken Dychtwald's message: 'I believe that by working on myself, I put myself in the most vital position to truly change and improve our social, cultural and global forms, and flows. Since all my actions and interactions are extensions and projections of who I am, how I feel, and what I believe, the best I can do for the rest of the world is to be my most open, creative and loving me.'[2]

This attitude is inherent in the Systems approach to a problem, which concentrates on the living system as a whole and on its inter-actions with its environment. It does not look at the environment and work backwards. The thought of the widespread acceptance of the message lies behind the optimistic views of man's future, golfers included, expressed by such wise men as Aurobindo, Leonardo, Teilhard de Chardin and our old friend, Shivas Irons.

[1] Robert M. Pirsig *Zen and the Art of Motorcycle Maintenance*, p. 291
[2] Ken Dychtwald *Bodymind*, p. 261

## RECOMMENDED FURTHER READING


1) Greg Brodsky *From Eden to Aquarius*
2) Frances Moore Lappé *Diet for a Small Planet*
3) Cadwallader and Ohr *Whole Earth Cookbook*
4) Ken Dychtwald *Bodymind*
5) Tony Buzan *Use Your Head*
6) David Boadella *Wilhelm Reich: The Evolution Of His Work*
7) Jolan Chang *The Tao of Love and Sex*
8) *Sunday Times Colour Supplement* 1977 'Take a tip from the African – more fibre in your diet means better business'.
9) June Singer *Androgyny*

# *Chapter Eighteen*

## CONCLUSION

*'We cannot all be champions, still less can any of us hope to be a champion among champions, like Harry Vardon or your Tom Morris before him. But we can be golfers in the real sense of the word. We can get the good of the game, which is the great thing today more than at any other day.'*

As the argument of this book developed something supremely ironic began to emerge. Here is a book supposedly based on a Systems approach to the problem and characteristics of the open system (the golfing bodymind) and yet it ends up discussing in great detail a property which is fundamentally *un*characteristic of nearly all the other Systems in the complex natural hierarchy, the property of *awareness.*

As Systems philosopher, Ervin Laszlo points out 'To be a man is to have the almost unique opportunity of getting to know oneself and the world in which one lives.'[1]

However, it is from this ironic situation that there emerges what Laszlo[2] justifiably calls 'the supreme challenge': to develop in ourselves this peculiar uniqueness and yet at the same time to retain that delicate balance both internally and externally with every other system in the hierarchy.

This 'question of balance' has been looked at from a number of different angles. For the human system it seems to mean balance between mind and body, between planned action and spontaneity, action and passivity, the mechanistic approach and the Systems approach, between the male in us and the female in us, giving and receiving, saying 'yes' and saying 'no'. If these many balances to be

[1] E. Laszlo *The Systems View of the World,* p. 119
[2] Ibid, p. 120

achieved pose 'the supreme challenge' actually beginning to strike a balance successfully must constitute 'the supreme skill'.

Striking a balance is not merely a problem for the individual golfer it is a problem on the social level. In practice, this really means the golf club and it means giving a place to skills and aptitudes neglected by the game. It means singing and dancing and acting as well as meeting to discuss the philosophy and psychology of the game. It means practising body disciplines and meditating and, above all, it means to participate.

When golf clubs start to move in these directions, they will also multiply the opportunities for the golfer to develop his particular uniqueness, for it may well be that his potential and talent lie not on the golf course, but in keeping the members in good spirits on a Saturday night. It is our task to create in the golf club the right environment in which our different potentials can be nurtured and expressed.

On a theoretical level, the twin problems of human uniqueness and Systems balance seem to have been best outlined by the philosophy of Ervin Laszlo, with his call for a 'reverence for natural systems', and the psychology of Abraham Maslow, with his study of the 'farther reaches of human nature'. On the individual level, however, what these two wise men have done is simply to point to the means and to hint at what we and our communities can become. Whether we actually realize this potential in golf or any other sport or activity depends not on other people's wisdom but on our own wisdom, the wisdom of the golfing bodymind. Other people can suggest ways, it is only the individual himself who can tell whether that way is right for him. Initially this is not possible for, as Alexander warns, what is 'right' often actually feels 'wrong'. Ultimately, however, we are on our own, both in golf and life with only the body's inherent wisdom to act as guide. This book has, I hope, offered some insight into how we can develop what is needed to stand on our own when that time comes.

# APPENDIX I

The aim of the tips and drills outlined below is to help the golfer overcome some of the mental blocks that prevent him from performing at his potential on the golf course. They are designed to narrow the gap between form on the practice ground and out on the course, between thought and action, between dreams and reality. They are *not* about the technical side of the game.

Some of the tips and drills are modifications of the work of the American tennis coach, Timothy Gallwey, the author of *The Inner Game of Tennis.* (Some readers may have seen him on the 'The Inner Game' film on BBC recently.) Other tips are based on our work with sportspeople in our 'Sporting Bodymind' workshops. The final source is from my work as a management consultant where we apply Synectics – an extensive and practical body of knowledge designed to help the individual and the group to their creative potential, and to release inherent problem-solving skills.

### *A) Drills for the Course or Practice Session*

These drills are best done with a friend, alternating playing and observing. It is important in these drills to observe the results of the shots without judging. Watch, listen and, most important, have fun.

#### I The Back/Hit Drill

This exercise is very simple. When you get to the top of your swing call out 'BACK' and when you hit the ball call out 'HIT'. Do it with a friend so that he can tell you whether your calling is accurate. The better the calling of BACK/HIT, the better the shot.

The theory behind this drill is to occupy the analytical, thinking mind (left hand side) during the performance of the shot. The assumption being that the bodymind knows how to hit the golfball if you keep the analysing mind out of the way.

II The Relaxation/Tension Drill
On a scale of 1 to 10 evaluate at the end of the shot how loosely or tightly you have gripped the club. Do the drill with a friend and call out the score after each shot. You will probably be surprised how loosely you can hold the club and may find that relaxing the grip leads to more power and a better shot. This drill should help to overcome the golfer's tendency to grip the club too tightly. Have you ever observed how loosely Jack Niklaus or Peter McEvoy seem to grip the club? In this exercise there is no right or wrong; simply observe and find out what works best for you. Before playing call out the score you intend to use and then compare with the actual. This drill is excellent for difficult chip or cut-up shots and putting.

III The Slow/Fast Tempo Drill
This drill is similar to the relaxation/tension drill in that the object is to measure on a scale of 1 to 10 the relative tempo and speed of the swing. There is no right or wrong in this exercise. It is designed to help the golfer discover his optimal swing speed and to experiment with different tempos. However, it is worth recalling Bobby Jones's assertion that it is not possible to swing the club too slowly.

IV The 'Club Head Path' Drill
In this drill, be aware of the club head as it travels through space while performing the shot. See how long you can stay with the path of the club head. Having done this for a while try doing the drill with your eyes shut.

This drill has two basic purposes. Firstly, it is an excellent exercise for improving concentration. I have found this exercise becomes considerably easier with practice. The second purpose is to improve awareness of both club head and swing.

V The 'As If' Drill
Select the top golfer whose swing or action bears most resemblance to yours or who you particularly admire. Recall, in as much detail as possible, this golfer going through the process of playing a shot and then act as if you were that golfer. Copy everything about him: his mannerisms, gestures, practice swings. Even try to imagine how that player feels during the performance of the shot. If you have a willing friend get him to pretend he is taking television pictures.

The principle behind this is the aphorism in pyschology that energy follows thought. It has been used by many successful people and I'm sure this is why it seems that the standard of golf is never better than during and after the British Open Week.

VI The 'Face/Mouth' Drill
You can tell a great deal about a golfer's state by observing the degree of tension in the face and particularly the mouth during his playing of the shot. Tension is reflected in the face. So just become aware of your face and mouth as you play your shot: notice whether or not your mouth is screwed up and watch the shot. Try this for ten shots on the practice ground and see what happens. This drill helps overcome golfing problem number one – anxiety. Anxiety and tension is a total mind/body state and cannot be isolated to one part of the body.

VII Sound Drill
The gap between thought and action is a significant one for many golfers. The main reason for this is that having done the analysing, thinking and, hopefully, imagining, prior to the shot, they continue the process during the performance of the shot, whereas they should be operating from the doing-acting mind (the right hand side of the brain).

One excellent way of making this transition from left brain to right brain is to use words or phrases which are said aloud as you play the shot. One suggested earlier was the Back/Hit drill. Here it is suggested that the golfer uses words with an onomatopoeic content – they sound like what you are trying to do. Try

a) Ooooommmmm – pah on back and forward swing respectively

b) A favourite tune, e.g. 'The Blue Danube'

c) A phrase, e.g. 'light arms and full swing'

d) A word, e.g. 'oily'

e) Make up words for particular situations e.g. in a bunker – 'splash' and 'splat' depending on whether the sand is dry or wet. Say out loud the phrase or word each time you play the shot. You may have to find a quiet corner of the practice ground but have a go!

B) *Drills and Tips for 'Off the Course'*

VIII The Evocative Words Technique
Psychologists are well aware of the fact that the words we use affect our moods. Research has shown that words affect both conscious

and unconscious minds. These insights can be used to improve your golf game. After all, Mohammad Ali has been using words to good effect since he started his phenomenal career. Apparently Harold Henning once looked into Player's room in the middle of the night when he heard a noise and found the South African in front of a mirror telling himself how good he was. The technique works as follows:

a) Select a word that expresses the quality you wish to evoke and develop in your golf – say calmness, concentration or consistency.

b) Write this word on a card and put it somewhere in your house where you will often see it (psychologists have found that even if we do not consciously notice the card it is having an effect on our mind).

c) Get in a state of relaxation and observe the word for a minute or two. If any ideas or images emerge from the unconscious let them come and record them.

d) Say the word out loud or murmur it repeatedly.

e) Write down the word many times.

IX The Slow Motion Visualization Technique

Top golfers are unanimous in stressing the importance of visualizing and imagining shots prior to their execution. Many psychologists are beginning to appreciate more fully the power and significance of visual rehearsal. It is particularly applicable to problems and ailments that do not lend themselves to the conventional golf instruction such as 'shanking' or 'twitching'. The technique works as follows:

a) Select a particular problem area on which you would like to work and choose a particular situation on your golf course where you have to execute the shot.

b) Find a comfortable position in which you can relax. Close your eyes and let go of any tension. (It has been found that visualization is very much more effective if the subject is relaxed.)

c) In your mind set the scene in vivid detail and in as many sense modalities as possible. This means imagining what kind of day it is, feeling the sun or wind against your skin, smelling the cut grass, seeing the cut of the green and seeing the colours of sand and green and sky.

d) Having set the scene it is time to rehearse in SLOW MOTION the particular shot that is causing problems. In many cases it is best to imagine yourself playing the perfect shot. However, if the fear surrounding this problem area is particularly intense you may find yourself unable to do this. We find in our workshop certain participants get a complete void or blank in certain aspects of their visual rehearsal. In this case it is important to visualize yourself with the defect to begin with. If emotions of fear or anger come up, avoid the tendency to fight them off and repress them. Try to accept and experience the emotion. If you repeat the visualization over and over the negative emotion associated with the shot tends to dissipate.

e) Rehearse the shot five times, each time resetting the scene in as much detail as possible. The real attraction of this particular technique is that it strengthens the golfer at his weakest point. Problems in one part of the game have a tendency to spread like a cancer, so overcoming those intractible golfing problems will tend to have a beneficial ripple effect on other aspects of your game. After all, they do say a chain is only as strong as its weakest link.

P.S. This drill is advisable when preparing for a round. We heard recently of the World Champion at trap shooting (the Olympic sport at which Britain's Bob Braithwaite won a gold in Mexico) who was to be seen prior to performing in a quiet spot, rehearsing mentally those parts of his performance which were causing him particular problems.

X Review Procedures – The Itemized Review

Many golfers do not review their game once they have completed a round. Often it is so painful we want to forget about it as soon as possible and head for the bar. This is unfortunate for there is much to be learnt from any round of golf whether good or bad.

I suggest you use an approach taken from my work in Synectics as a review procedure. This particular technique is described here as 'Itemized Review'.[1] Firstly, before you start criticizing your shot or round, you have to make three positive comments about it. Hence even a bad shot might warrant the following:

+ it went straight
+ it missed the bunker/out of bounds
+ it leaves me with an easy chip shot.

Forcing yourself to make these positives is going to leave you in a much better state of mind for the next shot than if you immediately start criticizing. Making three positive comments is important because the third tends to stretch the mind towards discovery – but one might be enough if you are feeling really bad about it, or, if three come easily, look for a fourth or fifth.

Next make the negative criticisms, but even these you must phrase in a constructive way by using a 'How to' statement. So rather than

[1] In Synectics terminology this is called an 'Itemized Response'.

stating 'What a terrible round' re-state it as 'How to play well after a heavy night' or 'How to keep trying after a bad start'.

An example of using the Itemized Review to a whole round is given in the following table.

*Itemized Review of a Round at St Andrews on 9 September 1979*

| | |
|---|---|
| + My chipping was excellent and the two bunker shots I had to hit were successful. | o How to organize myself better so I arrive in plenty of time to get in a bit of practice and arrive in an unflustered state on the first tee. |
| + I enjoyed the company of Mike and Joe. | o How to keep faith in the visual rehearsal of shots when I'm not playing too well. |
| + I hit an excellent drive on my dreaded bogey hole, the 17th. The mental practice I am doing at home seems to be paying off. | o How to overcome my fear of left to right putts and downhill putts |
| + I made a contract with Mavis (wife/girlfriend) to take her out for a meal tomorrow if she would let me play again on Sunday. I felt this eased my mind and helped me to concentrate on the golf – must do it again – she seemed to like the arrangement! | o How to retain control of my driving and long irons in a left to right wind. |
| | o I have two wishes for next time – a) to hole as many putts for birdies as I do for pars. b) to keep concentrating and trying whether the round is good or bad. |

## XI Concentration Tips

Practising concentration is just a question of selecting an object and focusing your attention on it for a period of time. The following suggestions may help:

a) Practice your concentration in a still and quiet place (e.g. the spare room or a corner of the garden). Try to use this place at the same time each day, for a fixed period to help build up associations with your previous practice sessions.

b) Find a symbol or picture which indicates stillness and calmness and which has some meaning for you. Leave it in this place.

c) Try doing some breathing and stretching exercises before beginning your concentration practice: perhaps yoga.

d) Sit erect. If you are unable to sit in a lotus position, it does not matter; a stiff-backed seat or placing a cushion under your backside is fine. You may wish to sit against the wall.

XII Keeping A Journal

This is a diary or notebook in which your thoughts concerning your golf and other aspects of your life are recorded. A journal is a valuable opportunity for self-reflection and helps to ensure that you move your game in the right direction. It also has the following, additional advantages:

a) It helps you focus on your game

b) Recording insights helps you remember them

c) Over a period of time you will see a pattern in your golf game

d) If you do it in terms of the Itemized Review described above, it will give you a more objective and constructive view of your game than you'd otherwise have.

# APPENDIX II

# *Yogic Breathing Exercises*

Golf is a game in which the player's feelings and emotions become totally engaged. While these are ordinarily very difficult to control, their destructive effects can be reduced through learning to use your breathing. Changing the pattern of the breath can automatically alter a mood. For example, an anxious person takes short, shallow breaths, but by learning how to take long slow, deep breaths, he or she finds that a feeling of calmness and confidence is induced with the change of breathing rhythm. The art of breath control not only helps one to control one's emotional states but improves concentration. Initially, however, breathing exercises do demand the application of a little concentration, but they are not difficult to practice and can be mastered in a very short time.

The exercises in this section are suitable for everyone, but follow the instructions carefully; do not overdo your practice and if you suffer from high blood pressure or have a heart condition, exercise with caution. If you should feel light headed or have vertigo, stop immediately.

Some of the exercises have a calming effect on the nervous system, others a stimulating effect which helps to clear the head and increase one's sense of well being.

EXERCISE I SECTIONAL BREATHING

This exercise can be practised lying down with the knees drawn up, sitting on the floor or in a straight-backed chair, or when standing.

a) Place the palms of your hands across the bottom of your ribcage with the middle fingertips meeting in the centre.
b) Close your eyes and bring your attention to rest beneath your hands. Without straining, inhale through your nose and attempt to 'fill up' the part of your ribcage covered by your

hands, so that the hands are pushed slightly apart. Exhale, feel the ribcage contract and the fingertips come back together again. Repeat twice.

c) Place your hands in the same way as described above over the middle of your ribcage just where your heart is. Take three breaths in the way instructed above.

d) Place your hands across your chest just under the collarbone. Take three breaths as above.

e) Return your hands to the bottom of your ribcage. Take in a small breath through your nose, expanding the lower part of the ribcage, pause while you move your hands to the middle of the ribcage, inhale a bit more, pause, move your hands to the chest, complete the inhalation, pause. Now reverse the process, exhaling, pause, move your hands to the middle section, exhale, pause, move your hands to the bottom of the ribcage and complete the exhalation. It is as if you are breathing in three short breaths and breathing out three short breaths. Pause and repeat twice more.

f) Keeping your hands over the bottom of the ribcage, inhale smoothly, 'filling up' the three sections. 'Empty' from the top down, feeling the chest, the middle section and the bottom contract smoothly. Repeat twice more, keeping the breath long and smooth.

g) Repeat the smooth breath through the three sections, but when

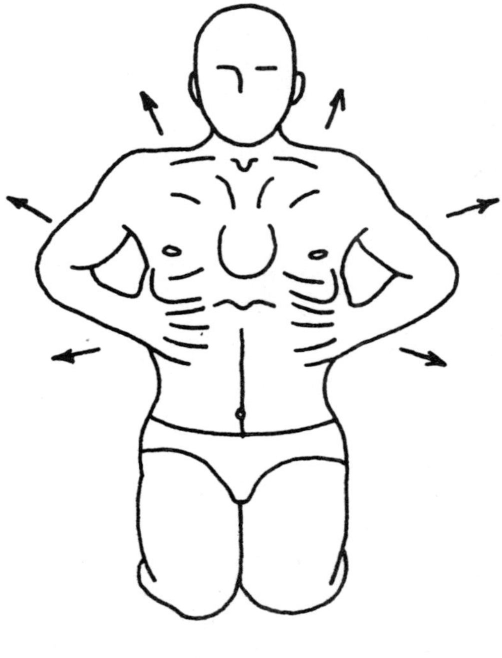

you have completed the inhalation, pause until you feel the *need* to breathe out. Then without straining, exhale smoothly through the chest, middle and bottom of the ribcage, pause and wait until you feel the need to breathe in.

Practice this sectional breath for a few minutes every day. Get into the habit of thinking of breathing up and down, rather than in and out. Feel the impetus for the in-breath begin from the bottom of the ribcage and the impetus for the out-breath begin in the chest. In between practice sessions, try to be aware of breathing as smoothly and effortlessly as possible in long, slow breaths which 'travel' up and down your ribcage.

EXERCISE II THE PELVIC TILT
This exercise helps to release tension, tones up the abdominal muscles and improves breathing in the upper lobes of the lungs.

a) Lie on the floor on your back. Bringing your legs together, bend your knees and place the soles of your feet on the floor as close to your buttocks as you can manage comfortably. Place your arms a little way away from your body and roll your hands over so that the palms are facing the ceiling.
b) Close your eyes and let your mind focus on your breathing. Breathe slow, complete breaths for a minute or so.
c) At the end of the next exhalation and keeping the lungs empty, contract your abdominal muscles, squeeze your buttocks together. Hold onto the contraction for as long as you feel comfortable, then let go and *allow* yourself to breathe in a complete breath. Follow it to the throat, pause, exhale and repeat the contraction.

Practise this exercise in rounds of three, taking three ordinary breaths without contracting the abdominal muscles between each round. Begin with six rounds and increase it slowly as the contraction becomes more effortless.

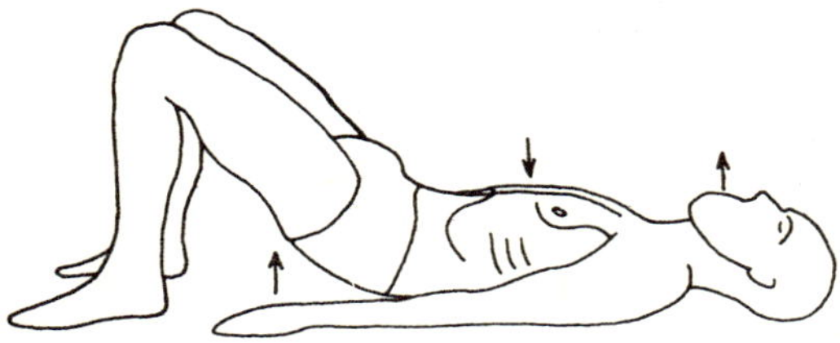

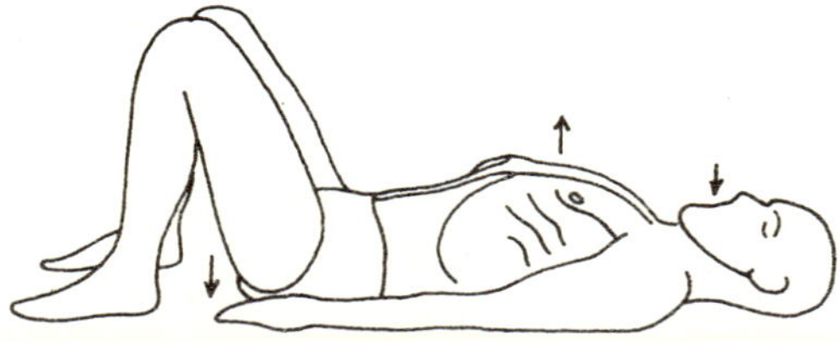

EXERCISE III THE MOUNTAIN

This exercise has a dynamic effect on the body, loosening the muscles of the chest and neck and strengthening the arms. It can be performed sitting in any position on the floor or in a chair provided the spine is kept erect.

a) Inhaling, raise the arms slowly with the breath until the palms meet overhead.
b) Exhaling, lower the wrists and rest them on the crown of the head.
c) Inhaling, move your hand about an inch off your head, exhale and rest. Inhale and move up another inch, exhale and rest. Repeat this process until the arms are fully stretched above the head.
d) Return by reversing the process, moving down on the exhalation, resting on the inhalation, until the wrists are once more on the crown.
e) Inhale, stretch the arms up fully; exhale and slowly, keeping the arms outstretched, return the arms to the floor then rest them, one on top of the other in your lap.
f) *Allow* yourself to inhale, without effort, a complete breath. Then sit, breathing quietly for about a minute before you get up or perform the next exercise.

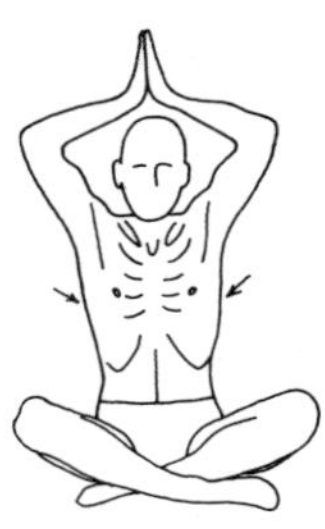

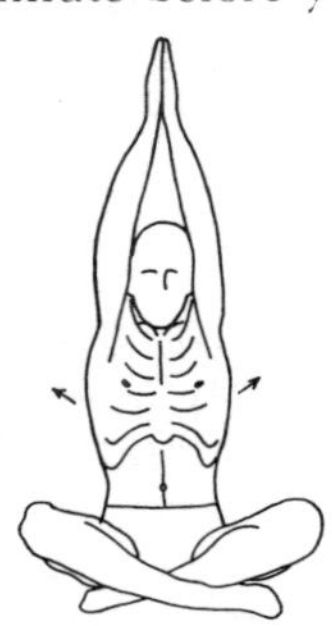

EXERCISE IV ALTERNATE NOSTRIL BREATHING

This exercise has a harmonising and balancing effect on the system.

a) Sit in any comfortable, straight-backed position.
b) Place the thumb against the right side of your nose, closing off the nostril. Place the index finger and middle finger in the centre of the forehead and close off the left nostril with the third finger.
c) Open the right nostril and inhale slowly, counting how long it takes to do so.

d) Close the right nostril with your thumb; hold the breath in for half the length of the in-breath; open the left nostril, exhale for the same length of time as the in-breath took, then close the nostril and hold the lungs empty for half the count.
e) Open the left nostril, inhale for the same count; close and hold for half the count; open the right nostril, exhale for the count, close and hold out for half the count.
This makes one complete round. Start with six rounds and increase it gradually. You can also increase your count with practice. If, for example your ratio is 4;2;4;2, increase it to 6;3;6;3, then 8;4;8;4; etc.

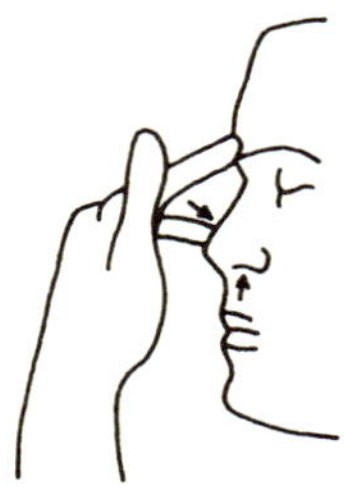

EXERCISE V THE 'HA' BREATH
This exercise has a cleansing effect and is believed to help increase confidence.

a) Stand with your feet about a metre apart and your hands on your hips.
b) Inhale a long, slow deep breath.
c) Exhale forcibly making the sound 'ha' as loudly as possible as you bend forward from the waist towards the floor.
d) Let yourself hang loosely without breathing for a few seconds.
e) Come up very slowly with the inhalation.
Repeat five more times.

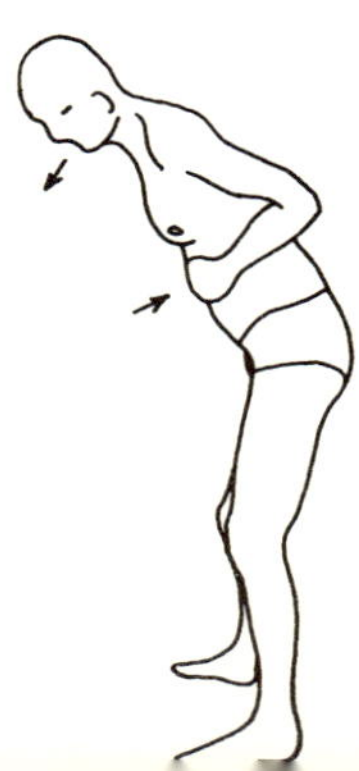

# APPENDIX III

## *The Sporting Bodymind*

Sporting Bodymind offers a new approach to sport based on concepts and themes of transpersonal psychology and the Human Potential Movement. Whereas sport has often been considered a contest between the mind and the body, with the mind struggling to direct, train and control a recalcitrant body, we suggest that the mind may be employed most effectively in building a co-operative relationship between itself, the body and the emotions. As this relationship becomes more harmonious, so does sporting performance improve.

Our courses are designed to show: (i) how the interrelationship of mind, body and emotions affects the sports person's attitudes and performance; (ii) how a lack of self-awareness will block the smooth co-operation of these three factors; and (iii) how the sports person can increase self-awareness and so fulfil his or her potential.

The distinction between the mind's intuitive, non-analytical understanding of how the body works and its ability to control and evaluate performance is clarified and we then examine the interplay of these two faculties. We find that when the proper use of the thinking evaluative function is balanced with increased sensitivity to the innate wisdom of the bodymind, not only does performance improve but our general sense of well-being is enhanced.

OBJECTS OF OUR WORK

1) To explore the interaction of the mind, body and emotions in sport.
2) To control anxiety and tension in stress situations.
3) To play more consistently under pressure.
4) To gain insight into sports motivation and achievement.
5) To explore 'peak experiences' in sport.
6) To enhance individual awareness and fulfilment of potential in sport.

PRINCIPLE METHODS

*Biofeedback* We receive a constant stream of messages from the body. Learning to hear these messages and responding appropriately is crucial if we are to improve our performance in sport and cultivate a fruitful partnership between our body and mind. Biofeedback techniques are numerous and range from simple exercises which can be done anywhere to the use of sophisticated Biofeedback machinery which amplifies and codifies the body's activities.

*Visualization* The use of visualization in sport has become increasingly widespread. Its effectiveness has been demonstrated by the U.S. Olympic ski teams, the U.S. biathlon team, the practice of world-class golf players and recently by the British Olympic trap shooters. Visualization techniques can be used to control anxiety, tension and fears in preparation for as well as during performance. It is also effective in motor skills training.

*Psychosynthesis* Psychosynthesis integrates a number of different techniques and methods under one comprehensive theoretical framework. Of particular relevance to the sports person is the work with mental imagery and the integration of conflicting aspects of the personality.

*Gestalt* Recurring obstacles to the sports person are self-recrimination about past mistakes and fears concerning future shots or games. These preoccupations with past and future performance detract from total attention on the task at hand. Gestalt shows how we take our attention away from the present and then helps us focus on the here and now.

*Body Awareness* Sporting Bodymind draws on yoga, Feldenkrais, Gurdjieff-school movements, aikido, juggling, sacred dance and other techniques designed to focus attention of the interaction of body, mind and emotions.

LEADERS

*Christopher Connolly* (31) has a B.A. from the University of Michigan and was on the staff of the Findhorn Foundation for five years. He has extensive experience in running groups and is now engaged in post-graduate work in humanistic psychology. An all-round sportsman and yoga student, his current research relates the use of guided imagery and visualization to physical therapy as a means of re-educating the body toward more constructive patterns of action and movement.

*Sandy Dunlop* (27) has a business degree from Trinity Dublin and is currently working for his M.A. in humanistic psychology. He is working with Abraxas Management Research as a management consultant on problem solving and creativity in business. He is a scratch handicap golfer and was Irish Youth, West of England and Gloucester Champion. He was reserve for England in 1976.

*John Syer,* M.A., M.Litt. (42) played hockey for Scottish Command and volleyball for Great Britain. He was National Coach and Director of the Scottish Volleyball Association for ten years, before joining the Findhorn Foundation in 1976. He spent part of 1979 on a staff-exchange visit to the Esalen Institute in California. A yoga teacher, he is concerned with the links between sport and meditation. His coaching, teaching and group leadership experience account for his particular interest in team performance as related to synergy and group dynamics.

NATURE OF WORK

The courses are a combination of lecture, practical work and discussion. We present certain principles which we then illustrate with practical exercises. Experience is a keynote and, while most of the course takes place in the meeting room, participants acquire specific skills and techniques which can be practised elsewhere. These techniques can be applied to any sport. They are designed to improve performance and to clarify the relationship between the player and his game.

The courses now offered in the London area include a one-day introductory course, and a two-day course. The Sporting Bodymind staff are prepared to offer additional courses both within and outside the London area. Individual consultancy is also available as a follow-up to the course and on an on-going basis.

For details of dates, places and costs, as well as expanded course description, write to

THE SPORTING BODYMIND,
Holcombe,
Weald Way,
Caterham,
Surrey

# BIBLIOGRAPHY


ALEXANDER, F. M., *The Use of Self,* Re-educational Publications, Manchester, 1957.

ALLPORT, G. W., *Becoming: Basic Considerations for a Psychology of Personality,* Yale University Press, London, 1955.

ARGUELLES, JOSE, *The Transformation of Vision: Reflections on the Nature and History of Human Expression,* Shambhala Pubns, Colorado, 1975.

ASSAGIOLI, ROBERT, *Psychosynthesis,* Turnstone, London, 1975.

ASSAGIOLI, ROBERT, *Act of Will,* Wildwood House, London, 1974.

BANNISTER, ROGER, *First Four Minutes,* Putnam, London, 1955.

BARLOW, W., *The Alexander Principle; How to use your Body,* Gollancz, London, 1973.

BERNARD, THEOS, *Hatha Yoga,* Rider, London, 1968.

BERTALANFFY, LUDWIG VON, *General Systems Theory,* Penguin, London, 1973.

BERTALANFFY, LUDWIG VON, *Robots, Men and Minds,* George Braziller, New York, 1969.

BOWDEN, GEORGE C., *F. Matthias Alexander and the Creative Advance of the Individual,* Fowler, Romford, 1965.

BRANDON, DAVID, *Zen in the Art of Helping,* Routledge and Kegan Paul, London, 1976.

BROWN, BARBARA, *New Mind, New Body,* Hodder and Stoughton, London, 1975.

BUHLER, CHARLOTTE, AND ALLEN, MELANIE, *Introduction to Humanistic Psychology,* Brooks-Cole, California, 1973.

CAMPBELL, DR DAVID, *If You Don't Know Where You're Going You'll Probably End Up Somewhere Else,* Argus Communications, Hoddesdon, 1976.

CAMPBELL, PETER A., *McMahon Edwin M. Religious Type Experience in the Context of Humanistic and Transpersonal Psychology,* Journal of Transpersonal Psychology, No. 1, 1974.

CAPRA, FRITJOF, *The Tao of Physics,* Wildwood House, London, 1975.

CASTENADA, CARLOS, *Journey to Ixtlan: The Lessons of Don Juan,* Bodley Head, London, 1975.

CASTENADA, CARLOS, *A Separate Reality: Further Conversations with Don Juan,* Bodley Head, London, 1973.

CASTENADA, CARLOS, *Teachings of Don Juan: The Yaqui Way to Knowledge,* Penguin, London, 1970.

CRAMPTON, MARTHA, *Psychological Energy Transformations: Developing Polarisations,* Journal of Transpersonal Psychology, No. 1, 1974.

DAY, HARVEY, *Yoga for the Athlete,* Kaye and Ward, London, 1974.

DURCKHEIM, K. G. VON, *The Way of Transformation: Daily Life as a Spiritual Exercise,* Allen and Unwin, London, 1972.

EMERY, F. E., *Systems Thinking,* Penguin, London, 1969.

FUERSTEIN, G., *The Textbook of Yoga,* Rider, London, 1975.

GALLWEY, T., *The Inner Game of Tennis,* Jonathan Cape, London, 1975.

GEBA, BRUNO, *Breathe Away your Tension: An Introduction to Gestalt Body Awareness Therapy,* Wildwood House, London, 1974.

GOLDSMITH, E., *The Stable Society,* The Wadebridge Press, Wadebridge, 1978.

GREEN, ELMER AND ALYCE, *Beyond Biofeedback,* Delacorte Press, New York, 1977

HERRIGEL, E., *Zen in the Art of Archery,* Routledge and Kegan Paul, London, 1972.

HICKMAN, JAMES L. Murphy, Michael, Spiro, Mike, *Psychophysical Transformations Through Meditation and Sport,* Simulation and Games, Vol.8 No.1, 1977.

HORNEY, KAREN, *Our Inner Conflicts,* Routledge and Kegan Paul, London, 1946.

HOUSTON, JEAN, *Re-Seeding America; The American Psyche as a Garden of Delights,* Journal of Humanistic Psychology, Vol. 18 No. 1, 1978.

HUANG, AL CHUNG-HAIG, *Embrace Tiger, Return to Mountain,* Bantam, London, 1977.

IYENGAR, B. K. S., *Light on Yoga,* Allen and Unwin, London, 1971.

JUNG, CARL G. *Modern Man in Search of a Soul,* Routledge and Kegan Paul, London, 1970.

KEEN, SAM, *To a Dancing God,* Collins, London, 1971.

KIRKALDY, ANDRA, *My Fifty Years of Golf, Memories,* T. Fisher Unwin, London, 1922.

LAO TZU, *Tao Te Ching,* Wildwood House, London, 1973.

LASZLO, ERVIN, *Introduction to Systems Philosophy. Toward a New Paradigm of Contemporary Thought,* Gordon and Breach, London, 1970.

LASZLO, ERVIN, *The Systems View of the World,* Blackwell, Oxford, 1975.

LEADBEATER, C. W., *The Chakras,* Theosophical Publishing House, London, 1927.

LEONARD, GEORGE, *The Transformation*, Dell, New York, 1972.

LEONARD, GEORGE, *Education and Ecstacy*, John Murray, London, 1970.

LEONARD, GEORGE, *The Ultimate Athlete*, Viking, New York, 1973.

LE SHAN, LAWRENCE, *How to Meditate: A Guide to Self-Discovery*, Wildwood House, London, 1976

LOWEN, ALEXANDER, *Bioenergetics*, Coventure, London, 1976.

MAISEL, E., *The Alexander Technique*, Thames and Hudson, London, 1974.

MALTZ, MAXWELL, *Psycho-cybernetics*, Wilshire Book Co, Los Angeles, 1967.

MASLOW, A. H., *Motivation and Personality*, Harper and Row, New York, 1970.

MASLOW, A. H., *Towards a Psychology of Being*, Van Nostrand Reinhold, New York, 1969

MASLOW, A. H., *Farther Reaches of Human Nature*, Penguin, London, 1973.

MAY, ROLLO, *Love and Will*, Fontana, London, 1972.

MILLER, JOHNNY, *Pure Golf*, Hodder & Stoughton, London, 1977.

MORLEY, DAVID, *The Missing Links: Golf and the Mind*, Atheneum, New York, 1976.

MURPHY, MICHAEL, *Golf in the Kingdom*, Sphere, London, 1976.

MURPHY, MICHAEL, *Sport as Yoga*, Journal of Humanistic Psychology, Vol. 17 No 4, 1977.

NICKLAUS, JACK, *Golf My Way*, Heinemann, London, 1974.

ORNSTEIN, R., *The Nature of Human Consciousness: A Book of Readings*, W. H. Freeman, Reading, 1973.

ORNSTEIN, R., *The Psychology of Consciousness*, W. H. Freeman, Reading, 1973.

PEALE, NORMAN VINCENT, *The Power of Positive Thinking*, Cedar Books, Tadworth, 1963.

PIERCE, JONES F., *Body Awareness in Action*, Schocken Books, 1977.

RAMA, BALLENTINE AND AJAYA, *Yoga and Psychotherapy*, Himalayan Institute, Illinois, 1976.

RAM DASS, BABA, *Be Here Now*, Lama Foundation, New Mexico, 1971.

RAVIZZA, KENNETH, *Peak Experiences in Sport*, Journal of Humanistic Psychology, Vol. 17 No 4, 1977.

RENDEL, PETER, *Introduction to the Chakras*, S. Weiser, New York, 1974.

REPS, PAUL, *Zen Flesh, Zen Bones*, Penguin, London, 1971.

ROHE, F., *The Zen of Running*, Random House, New York, 1975.

ROPP, ROBERT S. DE, *The Master Game*, Allen and Unwin, London, 1969.

ROTENBERG, MORDECHAI, *Alienating Individualism and Reciprocal Individualism: A Cross Cultural Conceptualisation*, Journal of Humanistic Psychology, Vol. 17 No 3, 1977.

ROWAN, JOHN, *Ordinary Ecstacy: Humanistic Psychology in Action*, Routledge and Kegan Paul, London, 1976.

SADHU, MOUNI, *Concentration*, Allen and Unwin, London, 1959.

SAMUELS, MICHAEL AND BENNETT, HAROLD, *The Well Body Book*, Wildwood House, London, 1974.

SAMUELS, MICHAEL AND SAMUELS, NANCY, *Seeing with the Minds Eye*, Random House, New York, 1976.

SCIENTIFIC AMERICAN, *Altered States of Awareness*, W. H. Freeman, Reading, 1972.

SINGER, JUNE, *Androgyny: Towards a New Theory of Sexuality*, Routledge and Kegan Paul, London, 1977.

SPANGLER, DAVID, *Revelation: The Birth of a New Age*, The Findhorn Foundation, Moray, 1971.

SUZUKI, SHUNRYU, *Zen Mind, Beginners Mind*, Weatherhill, New York, 1973.

TAIMNI, I. K., *Glimpses into the Psychology of Yoga*, Theosophical Publishing House, India, 1974.

TART, CHARLES T., (ED), *Altered States of Consciousness: A Book of Readings*, Wiley, Chichester, 1969.

TART, CHARLES T., (ED), *Transpersonal Psychologies*, Routledge and Kegan Paul, London, 1975.

TART, CHARLES T., *The Basic Nature of Altered States of Consciousness: A Systems Approach*, Journal of Transpersonal Psychology, No 1, 1976

TRUNGPA, CHOGYAM, *Cutting through Spiritual Materialism*, Robinson and Watkins, London, 1973

TRUNGPA, CHOGYAM, *Meditation in Action*, Stuart and Watkins, London, 1969.

VAN, LYSBETH, *Yoga Self-Taught*, Allen and Unwin, London, 1975.

WHICH PUBLICATIONS (ED. RUDINGER), *Avoiding Back Trouble*, Consumers Association, London, 1975.

WILBER, KEN, *The Spectrum of Consciousness*, The Theosophical Publishing House, 1977.

WILSON, COLIN, *New Pathways in Psychology: Maslow and the Post Freudian Revolution*, Gollancz, London, 1972.

WOOD, ERNEST, *Concentration; A Practical Course*, Theosophical Publishing House, 1949.

YESUDIAN, S., AND HAICH, E., *Yoga and Health*, Allen and Unwin, London, 1966.